# DENMARK IN THE EARLY IRON AGE.

# DENMARK

IN

# THE EARLY IRON AGE,

ILLUSTRATED BY RECENT DISCOVERIES

## IN THE PEAT MOSSES OF SLESVIG.

By CONRAD ENGELHARDT,

LATE DIRECTOR OF THE MUSEUM OF NORTHERN ANTIQUITIES AT FLENSBORG.

WILLIAMS AND NORGATE,

14, HENRIETTA STREET, COVENT GARDEN, LONDON, W.C.

20, SOUTH FREDERICK STREET, EDINBURGH.

1866.

LONDON.
VIRTUE AND CO., PRINTERS
294, CITY ROAD.

TO

HER ROYAL HIGHNESS

THE PRINCESS OF WALES,

THIS WORK

ON THE ANTIQUITIES OF HER NATIVE COUNTRY

IS

BY GRACIOUS PERMISSION

MOST GRATEFULLY AND RESPECTFULLY DEDICATED,

BY

THE AUTHOR.

# PREFACE.

THE following pages are principally devoted to a description of two great deposits of antiquities discovered in the peat-mosses of Thorsbjerg and Nydam, in South Jutland (Slesvig). They were excavated under my superintendence during the summers of the years 1858 to 1863, at the expense of the Danish Government, and incorporated with the then existing museum of Danish antiquities at Flensborg, of which they formed the chief ornament.

In one of these mosses the works were still unfinished when the two Allied German Powers, in the heart of the winter of 1864, assailed Denmark and conquered South Jutland. Peaceful occupations were then sadly interrupted; many of the inhabitants—and I amongst their number—had to leave house and home on account of their loyalty to their lawful sovereign: the systematic investigation of Nydam moss had to be discontinued, and the subsequent excavations at that spot, undertaken by German Princes and by a Prussian Baron, do not seem to have been carried on with the necessary care and intelligence.

Although, therefore, the investigation of one of these two great South Jutland moss-deposits cannot be considered as complete, the results obtained are nevertheless highly interesting and instructive, not only because these deposits contained so large a number of objects, which in both cases may safely be assumed to be almost contemporary, but also because they can be assigned with certainty to the earliest dawn of Danish history, when Iron first makes its appearance as being in general use in the

North, not indeed manufactured in a rude or imperfect manner, but treated with a technical skill and perfection, for which credit would not be given to the "barbarians" of the North of these remote times (the third century after Christ), if it were not for such unmistakeable proofs. Nor did we hitherto possess certain and indisputable evidences from so early a period of the use of the horse in the North for riding and driving, nor of the existence of skilfully-built boats, as the only existing boats of so ancient a date are, so far as I know, those discovered in Nydam.

I have attempted, through a description of these discoveries and a general survey of the principal contemporaneous remains hitherto discovered in other ancient Danish provinces, to give a picture of the remarkable and highly-developed state of civilization, which existed in Denmark in the Early Iron Age, such as may also have an interest beyond the boundaries of my native country.

One of the chief peculiarities of that period consists in a certain foreign civilizing influence, and I have accordingly made it an object of special attention to distinguish, as sharply and clearly as possible, between those antiquities which are plainly of Roman origin, such as the bronze helmet, the coins, etc., and those which are not Roman, but belong to a "barbarian" civilization, as, for instance, the silver helmet; and the result arrived at is, that the vast majority of objects dating from this period show absolutely no evidence of Roman influence. At the same time, I am perfectly aware of the difficulties involved in this attempt, owing to the scantiness of our information on the doubtless often very curious mixture of taste and style of workmanship, not less than habits and customs, which could not but arise along the extensive frontiers of the Roman Empire, from the daily intercourse—warlike or peaceful—between Romans, Romanized barbarians, and more or less barbarous tribes; and the difficulty is aggravated by our still greater ignorance of the arms and implements, technical skill and general habits of life of the so-called "barbarians,"—subjects on which Roman authors afford us remarkably little information. I trust I may be permitted to hope that on the present occasion I have succeeded in rendering to Cæsar the things that are Cæsar's.

Every statement occurring in this work as to how the objects were placed in the peat, their connexion, and state of preservation, are founded on my own personal observations, unless the reverse be expressly stated. I have been present at the extraction of almost every single object, and most of them I have taken out of the peat with my own hands. The Danish Government, by its liberal support and the interest which it took in the whole matter, rendered it possible to continue the excavations during six consecutive years, whenever circumstances were favourable. Thus only could these excavations yield so much as they did, and only thus could time be gained for hardening the wooden remains and for carrying out the often very difficult works of restoration.

It may, perhaps, interest the reader to know a little about the way in which these works were conducted. It is a fortunate peculiarity of the peat-mosses of the early Iron period,—if I may be allowed to describe them thus,—and one in which they coincide with the Swiss Lake-dwellings, that the antiquities lie together on a circumscribed area, instead of being scattered all over the moss or lake. When, therefore, any antiquities have been discovered in such a place by the peat-cutters, it will generally repay the trouble to examine the locality to see if they form part of a large hoard of the kind here described. Spade and shovel should be used only to a depth of one or two feet above the level where antiquities begin to appear; from that point they should be laid aside, as well as the heavy boots of the workmen, and only the hands used. It is preferable at once to prepare a tolerably large area for examination, as it is very difficult to begin at one of the sides without destroying something. According to the width of the surface of peat that has been cleared, five, six, or as many as convenient, of the most intelligent and cautious workmen that can be found, are set to work scraping away the soft soil from the top with their hands, as far as they can reach, looking sharp all the while that small objects do not escape between their fingers. Thus they proceed, clearing away one bank after another to the requisite depth; say, about one foot below the lowest point in which antiquities are found. Whoever superintends the work must be constantly present, and lend a hand if necessary. A clumsy person may sometimes, when not watched for a moment, damage and destroy an object which might have been saved, though no doubt, when the workmen perceive how much their care and caution is appreciated, it occurs more rarely that anything is lost; and after a few days, when they have learnt to recognize the more common objects,—as shields, swords, bows and arrows,—they also take particular pleasure in extracting, safe and entire, these fragile objects which are saturated with water. It is only by this method of proceeding, and by packing at once everything in soft peat, that so many and such fragile objects, which we could not expect to find preserved except in the mosses, have been saved from both these deposits, and preserved exactly in the state in which they were discovered. It is difficult always to be sure of having examined the whole area in which antiquities are found, because the soft semi-liquid peat substance obliterates the boundaries of the different trenches. It is therefore advisable to ˙push the examination a little beyond these boundaries.

I have, in conclusion, to record my sincere thanks to Mr. John Evans, F.R.S., Mr. J. Wickham Flower, Mr. C. A. Gosch, of the Danish Legation in London, and Professor G. Stephens, of the University of Copenhagen, to all of whom I am variously indebted for many valuable suggestions, and for kind assistance in the translation of my work and in seeing it through the press.

C. ENGELHARDT.

*Copenhagen, January,* 1866.

# CONTENTS.

————◆————

# DENMARK IN THE EARLY IRON AGE.

## INTRODUCTION.

THE division of the prehistoric period of Denmark into three distinct ages, those of *Stone, Bronze,* and *Iron,* so named from the materials used for weapons and cutting implements at different stages of human civilization, was first proposed in 1836 by the late C. J. Thomsen, the celebrated Director of the Copenhagen Museum of Northern Antiquities. That this division, and the corresponding classification of objects of antiquity, really express the true mode of development of civilization in the Scandinavian countries—and indeed, with some modifications, in the greater part of Europe—is amply confirmed by the results of all subsequent archæological investigations. But although these three periods are in themselves quite distinct from one another, and well characterized by the use respectively of Stone, Bronze, and Iron, for certain purposes, it does not follow that all Stone objects are attributable to the Stone period, nor all Bronze objects to the Bronze period. There are, on the contrary, in our museums, numerous stone axes which have evidently been manufactured at a time when bronze tools were already in common use; and we possess a great many fibulæ and brooches of bronze, of patterns unknown to the people of the Bronze age, but belonging to the Iron age. At that time iron was exclusively used for weapons and cutting implements, but bronze still occupied a place in the workshops for ornaments on scabbards, shields, etc., just as in the Stone age, when stone was the material exclusively used for weapons and sharp-edged tools, bone and amber served for smaller and blunter tools and for ornaments; and just as wood, no doubt, at all times was extensively used for domestic purposes.

It is but natural to suppose that stone was the first material used by mankind for weapons and cutting tools, and if there could be any doubt of the existence of a primitive *Stone age,* when the use of metals was unknown, that doubt must have been entirely dispelled by recent discoveries. For not only do we find stone antiquities by the thou-

B

sand scattered all over the country, in the fields behind the plough, in the forests and in the peat bogs; but the contents of the most ancient grave-mounds, of the shell beds (*kjökkenmöddinger*), and, in some measure, the accumulations of rude stone implements found on the coasts (*kystfund*, ' coast-finds') raise that hypothesis to a scientific truth. Now the usual character of our tumuli agrees in all essential points with that of similar remains, not only in England, but also over a large part of the European continent. A mound of earth, of round or oblong shape, has been raised over a stone-chamber with large cap-stones, and of very different proportions of length, breadth, and height. In such chambers are found sometimes a single skeleton,—commonly in a sitting or rather bent posture,—but oftener the remains of many human bodies. In many instances they were apparently family burial-places, or perhaps common cemeteries for a whole tribe or village. A stone-chamber may contain as many as eighty skeletons, and several instances have occurred in which the remains of the dead had been arranged in two or three layers, separated by flat stones (" Osseous interment").* Weapons and implements of stone and bone, amber beads, and vessels of burnt clay, made by hand without the help of the potter's wheel, and decorated in a peculiar and characteristic manner, are commonly found with these skeletons.

Of shell-mounds no less than about one hundred and fifty are known in Denmark. Some of these have been partially examined by a committee appointed for that purpose, consisting of Professors Forchhammer, Steenstrup, and Worsaae. They consist of large heaps of refuse from the food of the people of the Stone age. The shells of oysters and other edible *testacea*, bones of fish and game, and fragments of pottery of burnt clay, are mixed up together, and among these essential constituents of the shell-beds are found a quantity of simple and rude implements of stone and of bone, which have evidently been either dropped by those who took their meals in the vicinity of the heaps, or thrown away as useless.

That the tumuli with stone implements and the shell-beds alike belong to the Stone age is undoubted, but the Danish Archæologists do not agree upon the important question whether they are contemporaneous or not.

One of the members of the above-named commission, Professor J. J. A. Worsaae, has advocated a division of the Stone age into an *earlier period*, to which are ascribed the remains from the heaps and coast-finds, and a *later period*, to which belong the well-finished objects found in the stone chambers of the tumuli. Another member of the commission, Professor J. Steenstrup, is, on the contrary, of opinion that all these remains *may* be contemporaneous, seeing that, as he asserts, some fragments of ground and finished stone implements have been found in some of the heaps, and that at the same time implements of certain descriptions, supposed to be characteristic of the shell-mounds, are doubtless also met with in graves along with the more finished

* Similar stone-chambers on the Channel Islands have been explored and described by F. C. Lukis. See his ' Observations on the Celtic Megaliths, etc.' in the Archæologia, vol. xxxv. 282.

articles usually found there. The first of these facts would, of course, if satisfactorily established, afford a decisive proof against the proposed division of the Stone age, nor would the rarity of such highly-finished implements in the shell-beds detract from the force of the argument; inasmuch as we could of course not expect to find them there unless when lost by accident. It may also be observed that the highly-finished appearance of the beautiful specimens of axes, etc., often found in the graves, is in a great measure owing to their being ground, whilst the rude implements of the shell-beds are merely chipped off the core or block of flint; but the former process is much easier than the second, and does not by any means presuppose a higher state of civilization.

The question, however, is not yet definitely settled. The contents of the graves have not been examined with sufficient minuteness in all cases, and much remains to be done in this respect as in many others. But even if these relics of the oldest known civilization in Denmark were proved to be of different dates, the next step would be to decide which of them was the earlier, for it does not necessarily follow that the ruder period must be the older. There may have been a period of degradation in the Stone age, as there certainly was in after times,—for instance, from the third century after Christ to the middle ages.

During the *Bronze age* swords, poniards, and other cutting implements were almost exclusively made of bronze by the process of casting. The metal is a mixture of nine-tenths of copper and one-tenth of tin. Though axes of massive bronze occasionally occur, stone axes were still in use for domestic and other purposes, they were not only as useful in many cases as bronze axes, but the material was certainly cheaper. Gold was extensively used for personal ornaments, for bracelets and finger-rings of the spiral form, for twining round the hilts of swords, or ornamenting hair-pins and other articles of the toilet. But among the many proofs of the inferior civilization of this age as compared with the ensuing period—the Early Iron age—we may mention the ignorance of the use of iron, the want of a written alphabet, and, for manufacturing purposes, ignorance of the art of soldering.

Objects of art in a stricter sense—imitations of human and animal forms—were not wholly unknown, it would seem, at that time, but they occur very seldom. Among the many thousand antiquities of the Bronze age, found in Denmark, and preserved in the museums, only five or six are of this kind. Specimens are represented in Worsaae's 'Northern Antiquities,' fig. 167 (a swan), 171 (a fish), and 166 (a man holding a vessel in his hands).

Various modes of sepulture were practised in Denmark during this period. In many cases, the dead were buried in large coffins hollowed out of solid trunks of oak from seven to ten feet in length. The body wrapped in woollen clothes was laid in a hide, and weapons were deposited along with it, as well as wooden vessels decorated with tin pins, combs of bone, and tweezers of bronze. These oak coffins are found in tumuli, and about twenty instances of such interments are known in Denmark, besides some in Great Britain. Mr. Williamson, in 1834, published a description of a tumulus at Gristhorpe, near Scarborough, in which a discovery of this kind was made.[*]

Of rarer occurrence, perhaps, than these hollowed trunks, are cists of stone,—somewhat resembling the stone chambers of the earlier period,—of the length and breadth of a human body, and covered either with flat stones or with boards, the remains of the latter being sometimes still traceable in the earth.

In most cases, however, the bodies of the dead were burned, and the remains collected into urns of burnt clay, and it is a very remarkable fact that such urns have very frequently been buried in the sides of barrows belonging to the preceding or Stone age, as is proved by the contents of stone-chambers in their interior. Commonly the urns have been placed on a flat stone, and surrounded by smaller stones, leaving just room enough in the middle for the urn, which, however, in many cases is without this protection. Among the burnt bones contained in such vessels, some small bronze objects, such as knives, fibulæ, tweezers, etc., are often found. We may, perhaps, look upon these graves as the burial-places of the humbler classes.

Lastly, there are not a few barrows, which have not only been used as burial-places by the people of the Bronze period, but also owe to them their origin. These barrows are commonly as large as those of the Stone age, and contain in the centre an urn, filled with burnt bones, and surrounded by small stones, forming a little heap for its protection.

In such burial-places, as well as in fields and peat bogs, objects are found characteristic of the age of Bronze—such as garments, weapons, and musical instruments, personal ornaments, implements and household utensils, articles of the toilet, and vessels of gold and bronze. These objects never bear inscriptions, and are but very rarely ornamented with representations of animals; nor have, so far as I know, horse-trappings, or other evidences of the use of the horse, been met with among the antiquities of the Bronze period.

Comprised within the *Iron age* of Denmark three subdivisions may be clearly distinguished,[†]—the Early Iron age from about 250 to 450 A.C., the Transition period, extending to the close of the seventh century, and the Late Iron age, terminating with the introduction of Christianity about the year 1000.

The Early Iron age, with which we are here now particularly concerned, presents at its very first appearance three important elements of a higher civilization: the use of iron, of horses for riding and driving and of an alphabet of Runic letters, and technical skill is evinced to a degree which must excite our wonder and admiration,

---

[*] Compare Sir R. Colt Hoare's 'Ancient Wiltshire,' vol. i. 122, etc., Wilson's 'Archæology of Scotland,' p. 462, and 'The Reliquary,' vol. v. 1.

[†] J. J. A. Worsaae's 'Northern Antiquities,' 1854, where this classification was first established in its main features, and the same author's 'Antiquities of South-Jutland, or Slesvig,' 1865.

accustomed as we have been from our youth to look upon all ancient races, except the Greeks and Romans, as "uncivilized barbarians." Weapons and cutting instruments were invariably made of iron, the manufacture of which had reached a high state of perfection at the time of its first appearance in Denmark, and instead of the cast bronze sword of the previous age, we suddenly meet with damascened and welded swords of iron. The two other metals, mentioned above as being already known during the preceding period, were also used in this; but the bronze, or rather brass, was now differently composed, zinc being mixed with the copper instead of tin. Gold also occurs in massive rings, as well as in very thin plates, for the decoration of various objects. Besides these metals, silver was extensively used in massive pieces, as well as in thin plates, covering articles of bronze, and thus giving them a more costly appearance. Ivory, glass, agate, and beads of variegated porcelain also make their first appearance in this period.

Instead of the geometrical and somewhat stiff and monotonous ornaments which are characteristic of the works of the foregoing period, we now find a livelier and more artistic ornamentation, consisting of human figures, serpents' heads, dragons and crocodiles, birds and other animals, stars, pearls, the fylfot (卐),* and many others. The graceful appearance usually given to objects of meaner materials by means of ornamental plates of silver and gold, and their pure style of decoration and shape which evidently belong to a highly-civilized people, make this period the richest and most interesting of our prehistoric times.

A comparison between the woven fabrics of the Bronze age† and those of the Early Iron age (Thorsbjerg, Plates 1 and 2) will give a very good idea of the advance of art in this respect in the latter period.

The horse was, as stated above, probably introduced into Denmark, in a state of domestication, at the same time as iron. For although numerous bones of horses have been found in the lake-habitations of Switzerland, of the Bronze period,‡ from which we might be inclined to infer that this noble and useful animal was not unknown to the contemporaneous tribes of the North, yet neither in the Stone nor the Bronze age do we find any remains of this animal, nor any horse-trappings.

The size and build of boats of oak and fir, found in Nydam Moss, show that the men of that time were far advanced in the art of constructing sea-going vessels.

But the greatest proof of the higher degree of civilization prevailing in Denmark during the Iron age is to be found in the fact that the people of that time possessed an alphabet. Art was not wholly unknown to the people of the preceding ages, but

---

* In a notice on the religious Star-, Cross- and Circle-Symbols of the Ancients, by Dr. L. Müller, lately published in the Transactions of Videnskabernes Selskab, vol. iii. 5th series, the sign is said to have originated in Eastern Asia, from whence it spread over a great part of Europe, symbolizing, with northern nations, Odin as the fast-running, the all-penetrating god.

† See Sir John Lubbock, 'Prehistoric Times,' p. 27.    ‡ *Ibid.* p. 145.

no alphabetical characters of any kind have ever been discovered on any objects that belonged to them. Of these Old-Northern Runic Inscriptions more will be said hereafter, but they have not yet been satisfactorily explained. Professor G. Stephens, of Copenhagen, is engaged on a detailed account of them, with facsimiles and alphabets, and his work will doubtless throw much light on the whole subject.

Mixed up with the other remains of that time, a greater or less number of objects of Roman origin is often found, thus proving that the people who deposited the objects, and to whom the majority of them are to be attributed, had at some time or other, either directly or indirectly, intercourse with the Romans. They have even been influenced by this Latinizing contact so far as to adopt Roman letters for native names such as RICVS, RICCIM, COCILLVS, TASVIT, etc., stamped in raised letters on tangs of iron swords from Nydam and Vimose; but this seems to have been only a passing fashion, and there are no traces of Roman influence in the objects of art. The Romans, we know, never conquered Denmark. Their armies, assisted by their fleets, came as far as the Elbe, but never beyond it ; Roman antiquities, therefore, rarely occur alone in Denmark, nor has a single Roman sepulchre been met with, as in England and other countries which once felt the yoke of the world-conquering nation. Such antiquities are here almost always discovered in connection with what we may call our native antiquities, and it is very important to direct attention to a proper separation of these two classes of objects.

After this rapid sketch of the different stages of progress, of which our antiquities give evidence, until about the middle of the fifth century, we have to consider the important question, whether there are connecting links between the three periods, and whether the same people has always lived in this country, so that we, the Danes of the nineteenth century, may call the people of the Stone age our ancestors, or whether we are the descendants of more recent invaders ? Have the changes which we have endeavoured to indicate taken place gradually, or have new nations, provided with better arms, and more highly civilized, poured into the country and subdued or driven away the original inhabitants ? As bearing on this point we may observe that unburnt bodies and stone objects have but rarely been discovered in connection with bronze. Such cases might indicate a transition period between the Stone and the Bronze ages, but they may perhaps more properly be assigned to a late period of the Stone age, when tribes of the stone-using people had become acquainted with weapons and implements of metal, though as yet the civilization of the Bronze age had not made the inhabitants alter their ancient mode of sepulture. For it must be borne in mind that the latter age was one of cremation, principally, though not exclusively; while in the former period, the bodies of the dead were invariably buried unburnt. It is difficult to imagine such a great and important change being brought about only by pacific intercourse and commercial relations with nations of higher civilization.

Nor would such an explanation, in my opinion, satisfactorily account for the transition from the Bronze to the Iron age. The differences are too striking; we look in vain for points of resemblance between the antiquities of the two periods with regard to shape and ornamentation. We have, for instance, at present in Denmark about one hundred and seventy swords of the Early Iron period, and about three hundred and fifty swords of the Bronze period; but among these rich stores we do not find a single connecting link between the sword of cast bronze, and that of welded and damascened iron. We find, moreover, in the Iron age, new ornaments as well as new materials, and a different composition and treatment of those formerly known. If a gradual and organic transition had taken place between the two ages, we should naturally expect in objects of art—such as representations of men and animals—to see the first feeble attempts of art in its infancy. But that is not the case. The objects of this kind belonging to the Early Iron period (Thorsbjerg, Plate 7, Fig. 7, and Plate 11, Fig. 47, among many others) are barbarous enough, but they are far from representing art in its infancy. We observe, on the contrary, a decline of art from its comparatively high development in the early period of the Iron age to a much lower standard towards its conclusion, with regard to style and form, as well as to technical skill in metal-work.

For these reasons, on the last of which I am inclined to lay peculiar stress, we are, in my opinion, justified in assuming, that the higher state of civilization was the result of an invasion, for in no other way can the sudden appearance of damascened weapons, of materials hitherto unknown, of horses, arts, and letters, be satisfactorily explained.

From the great number of remains,* it appears certain that each of the three great periods must have comprised many centuries, but it is impossible to say how far we are to go back to find the commencement of the Bronze period, much less that of the Stone age. The question cannot be solved by the antiquities themselves, for of coins and inscriptions there are none of those early times to assist us. We may infer from the respective position of the burial-places, that the Bronze age followed after the Stone age, but we do not know when the change took place.

With regard to the Early Iron age in Denmark, which the present work is specially intended to illustrate, and which has a double interest to the Danes, being the dawn of our national history, we have much better means of judging, since coins and objects of art are trustworthy guides for fixing dates. The Roman coins from all the deposits are of the second and the beginning of the third century, as are also the objects of art of Roman origin. Thus we are enabled to conclude with certainty that these deposits cannot be older than the third century of the Christian era. At that time, the civilization which characterizes this period was in the highest state of development in our country. It then gradually sank till about the fifth century, when other or modified forms with a style of ornamentation either in part or entirely new were introduced, probably in consequence of the great immigration of tribes from the East.

* The number of stone implements alone, preserved in public and private collections in Denmark, may be estimated at no less than 40,000; and how many have disappeared.

# CHAPTER I.

## GENERAL SURVEY
## OF DANISH ANTIQUITIES OF THE EARLY IRON AGE.

THE Early Iron age in Denmark has been so fully and minutely illustrated by the discovery of large deposits of antiquities, that little doubt is left as to what objects must be referred to it. They have been brought to light in great numbers from burial-places, from hoards or hiding-places in the earth, and especially from peat-bogs or mosses. In the accompanying map of Denmark, about two hundred localities are indicated, in which objects of this age have been discovered. These finds may be divided into several classes, distinguished by different signs in the map, viz. :—

1st. Graves with bodies unburnt.
2nd. Burial-places with remains of burnt bodies.
3rd. Finds of objects accidentally lost or intentionally deposited in the earth.
4th. Moss deposits.
5th. Finds of Roman coins.

### A.

It is evident, from the contents of the burial-places, that a people at this stage of civilization once spread over almost the whole country, and that two modes of sepulture were in use among them. Instances of *Cremation* rarely occur. No more than about twenty well-authenticated instances have come to our knowledge. Vessels of burnt clay,—in one case a bronze vessel, in another a glass cup,—contained the burnt human bones. Among the remains, bronze fibulæ of the Roman bowed form, tweezers of bronze, or some small iron object, proved the grave to belong to this age. Such sepulchral remains have never been found in mounds raised expressly for the purpose of protecting the grave and serving as memorials of the dead, as was the case during the two preceding ages. They are met with in the sides of older barrows and natural eminences. As an example of these burial-places, the relics from a barrow at

Bolderslev, near Aabenraa in Slesvig (a district rich in memorials of early times), are particularly worthy of notice (Map, Slesvig, No. 11). Names found in the Ancient Northern Mythology are here preserved, in the names of many localities, though often in a mutilated shape; legends connected with many of the barrows are still extant. Thus Bolderslev signifies the heritage or seat of Balder, the good and righteous god. Near this village a large barrow of about fórty feet in diameter, and twelve feet high, was opened a few years since. About four feet below the surface, two large urns of clay were found close together, both filled with burnt human bones. The largest of these vessels, resembling in shape the one figured in Thorsbjerg, Plate 17, No. 11, is about eleven inches high, and ornamented with the zigzag pattern. The smaller, eight inches high, is of the same shape as the larger one, and ornamented in the same manner. Among the burnt bones were found a bowed bronze fibula (like Thorsbjerg, Plate 4, No. 1), and a rusty piece of iron, probably the remains of a knife. At about two feet under this urn, the labourers came upon a grave of the Bronze age, a hollow formed of slabs of stone, and containing burnt bones, among which were a knife, an arrow-head, and a hair-pin, all of bronze. Common cemeteries, with mortuary urns containing calcined human bones, are by no means of rare occurrence, but it is rather difficult in most cases to determine their age, for they are usually unaccompanied by any antiquities, and the few objects that have been found are small and much corroded. Such urns, standing near each other, and filled with burnt bones, are to be met with, scarcely one foot beneath the surface, in waste and uncultivated fields, when the soil is broken for the first time.

The late Mr. Mecklenburg, of Flensborg, to whom the museum of his native city is indebted for many and important presents, has given an account of one of the most valuable of these cemeteries in the Proceedings of the Antiquarian Society of Kiel, for the year 1844, p. 33. In a sandy field at Smedeby (Slesvig, No. 21 on the map), between Flensborg and the town of Slesvig, about one foot beneath the surface, an astounding number of urns was found deposited, mostly on flat stones, sometimes surrounded on all sides by smaller stones, some covered with a flat stone.* The urns, in their general character,

Urn, from Smedeby. ‡

are not unlike many of those from Anglo-Saxon graves, though their style of ornamentation is somewhat different.† (See the accompanying chemitypes.) Among the burnt bones in the

Iron Knife, from Smedeby. ⅓.

* For similar deposits, see C. Roach Smith, Coll. Ant. vol. ii. 228.

† See J. M. Kemble, " On Mortuary Urns found at Stade-on-the-Elbe," Archæologia, vol. xxxvi. 270; and ' Horæ Ferales.' Compare also Akerman ' Pagan Saxondom,' p. 43. Urn found at Eye, Suffolk.

C

vases were found—fibulæ of bronze and iron, of the bowed Roman form, resembling those figured by Nos. 1, 2, and 4, in Plate 4; tweezers and earpicks (commonly suspended from one ring), knives of iron, similar to those represented in Akerman's Archæological Index, xv. nos. 9 and 10; shears of iron (*ibid.* xviii.). The only fragment indicating that weapons also had been thrown on the funeral pile, was a bronze clasp for the middle of a wooden scabbard, in shape somewhat like that figured in No. 29, Thorsbjerg, Plate 10, of this work. The half-burnt piece adhered to a massive iron ring, one and a half inch in diameter, and to the fragment of a human skull.

It appears from the contents of about forty *graves with skeletons*, that the common mode of burial was to deposit the body entire at full length, and commonly in the direction of south to north, the head towards the south, in gravelly soil, or on natural eminences, some four or five feet beneath the greensward. There are above-ground no indications of a grave, nor have usually any preparations been made beneath. In one case a grave had been dug in a clayey soil and filled with fine earth; others were found covered with larger stones, symmetrically arranged in this manner— ≋00≋ ; and there are also a few instances of chambers built of stone, and of about the dimensions of a human body.

It is very much to be regretted that almost all objects of this kind have been obtained by chance discoveries, and that none of the burial-places have been carefully examined. We are in consequence left in doubt on many important points connected with the graves. The burial-places discovered in gravel-pits seem mostly to have been family sepulchres. Five, six (and sometimes, in the words of the labourers, "many") skeletons are found side by side. At the sides of the skeletons, or upon them, sometimes in their arms, are found objects characteristic of this age. It is rare to hit upon a grave without a vessel of some description; usually one or two vessels are placed near the head, and some at the feet.* Besides pottery, vessels of bronze, bottles of glass, and wooden buckets, are found in the graves. The vessels of bronze and glass are mostly of Roman workmanship, some even of the best period. On the handles of the former, stamps with raised letters are often observable, though the exact letters can rarely be ascertained. The stamps on two vessels, not taken from the graves, have been deciphered. One has DIS⩚CVS F (Worsaae's Ant. no. 308); and another from Ringe, in Fyen, NIGELLIO F. On the other hand, bronze vessels of decidedly native, at least not Roman manufacture, are by no means uncommon. (Compare the chemitype, p. 14, bronze vase from Mollerup.) It is likewise uncommon to find a grave without a bronze-bound bucket of wood. The English reader will be familiar with the frequent occurrence of such objects among the contents of tumuli of a later date, the Anglo-Saxon period.†

* Specimens of similar vessels are figured in Worsaae's 'Antiquities,' Copenhagen, 1859, pp. 71 to 78. Only one of these, No. 318, is from a grave. For similar vessels found in England and Scotland, see 'Archæologia,' vols. x. 133, 169; xi. 105; xv. (plates xxxi. to xxxiii. and xxxvii.); xviii. 340; xxx. 182, etc.

† See, for instance, Neville's 'Saxon Obsequies,' pl. xvii.

We cannot say for what purpose the various vessels were deposited near the dead, but it seems at that time to have been an almost invariable custom; and, what is very curious, several instances are known of saucepans with the accompanying strainer, fitting exactly, having been discovered among the remains.

Although no instance has been recorded of any fragment of dress or cerecloth having been preserved in the tombs, the dead were doubtless attired for the grave in one way or other, for personal ornaments, as hair-pins of silver and bronze, finger-rings, beads, and fibulæ, are often dug up. The beads are made of clay, amber, glass, vitrified porcelain in variegated designs, and occasionally of spiral wire of gold, silver, or bronze. Almost all the finger-rings are of gold, and mostly of the spiral form; a good specimen is given in Worsaae's Ant. no. 382, found on one of the fingers of a skeleton. Fibulæ occur of bronze, silver, and gold, of the curved or circular form; the common shapes are shown in Worsaae's Ant. nos. 388, 389, and 390; costlier specimens in nos. 385 and 395.

Objects of the toilet are comparatively rare. Bone combs have been found by the side of four of the skeletons.

Shears of bronze and iron are sometimes brought to light.

Draughtsmen occur in glass and bone.

Weapons are comparatively few. Though this may in some measure be owing to the rapid decomposition of the iron in the moist soil, it does not appear to have been usual to deposit them at the dead warriors' side. Whether this may be ascribed to Roman influence, I cannot say. The facts are not yet sufficiently numerous and authentic to give a clear view of the subject. The few weapons from the graves perfectly resemble those which the mosses have yielded. (See the annexed figures.)

Bronze Boss, from Sösum; found near a human skeleton. (Map Sealand, No. 5.)

Bronze Boss, from Vigerslev; found on a skeleton. (Map Fyen, No. 8.)

C 2

Horse trappings are perhaps still more rare.

Two bronze spurs have been found like that represented in the accompanying figure.

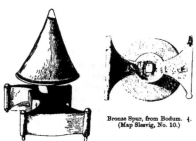

Bronze Spur, from Bodum. ¼.
(Map Slesvig, No. 10.)

In only three of the tombs were Roman coins met with, a silver coin (*denarius*) of Antoninus Pius, one of Lucius Verus, and a barbarous imitation of a coin of Geta.

Skeletons of horses were found along with human bodies in a cemetery near Aarhuus, in North Jutland (compare No. 2 hereafter); some bones of the tame goose, and of the pig (probably domesticated) were found near a human skeleton at Varpelev, in Sealand; the skeleton of an ox, along with a gold hair-ring with the inscription LVÞRO (probably to be read in two words LVÞR o(wns) ) in Runic letters, was found in a hill at Straarup, in South Jutland (map No. 1), among stones,—the remains, it was supposed, of a disturbed grave-chamber.

We have proofs of contact with the Romans in objects of Roman workmanship and with Roman inscriptions. One inscription is known in Greek letters on a crystal ball (Worsaae's Ant. no. 379). Evidences of the Gothic origin of many of the objects are, on the other hand, found in their workmanship and ornaments, no less than in names and other inscriptions in Runic letters.

The following brief descriptions of the whole contents of some characteristic graves belonging to this period, may serve to illustrate the matter more fully :—

1.

Near Bennebo, in the parish of Skamstrup, in Sealand (No. 22 on the map), were discovered on and near the remains of a human body.

Two fibulæ, one in brass, one in silver (compare Worsaae's Ant. 390 and 395);

A gold spiral finger-ring of six coils;

Fragments of a bronze vessel, resembling in shape Worsaae's Ant. fig. 302;

A saucepan and strainer, of bronze, like *ibid.* 309 and 310;

A silver coin, of Antoninus Pius, A.D. 145–147.

2.

In digging for gravel near Framlev, in the bailiwick of Aarhuus, Jutland (No. 23 on the map), the labourers came upon many human skeletons and many bones of animals, especially of horses, which appeared to have been buried with the bodies. By the feet of one of the latter stood a bronze-bound wooden bucket, at its head was a curved bronze fibula of the Roman form, on the breast about thirty beads of amber, glass, and variegated porcelain. In the same gravel mound, some members of the Society of Antiquaries at Aarhuus afterwards opened a grave, dug in the earth, and filled with a soil darker than the surrounding earth; length six feet, breadth four feet, depth five feet. In it was deposited a (female?) skeleton, the head towards the west, the legs bent up, and arms crossed. A necklace of small beads of amber, glass, and porcelain; three bronze fibulæ of the Roman form (like Fig. 1 in Thorsbjerg, Plate 4 of this work), and a bronze pin were found on the skeleton, at the side of which were placed numerous vessels of burnt clay, full of earth.

3.

In 1820, labourers in digging gravel on a rising ground near Aarslev, by Svendborg, in Fyen (No. 20 on the map), came upon two human skeletons—one, it was supposed, a male, the other, a female—four feet from each other, the heads towards the south. With them were found a wooden bucket and two bronze vessels, in one of which had been deposited a silver spoon (Worsaae's Ant. 304). On the female skeleton were dis-covered :—

Seven gold ornaments, set with garnets; one of them is represented in Worsaae's Ant. no. 393.

A costly gold fibula set with garnets and cornelians. (*Ibid.* no. 387.)

Another gold fibula, with ornamental grooves filled with lead. (*Ibid.* No. 386.)

A golden finger-ring with three garnets, closely resembling that figured in Wor-saae's Ant. no. 381.

Another finger-ring of the spiral form.

A crystal ball, with the inscription in Greek letters *ABΛΛΘΑΝΑΛΒΛ*, a magic word, probably, like Abracadabra. The ball was doubtless a Gnostic talisman.*

A gold coin, being a barbarous imitation of a coin of Geta, or of one of the later emperors.

The last-mentioned find probably belongs to the transitional period, between the Early and the Later Iron age. It corresponds in many points with remains found in Anglo-Saxon tombs.† The intertwined ornaments characteristic of the Late Iron age do not occur upon these objects, but the frequent use of set stones is one indication, among others, of inferior taste. The comparatively late date is moreover confirmed by the coin. The deposit from Bennebo, on the contrary, may be assigned to the second or third century A.C. The two discoveries accordingly determine the beginning and the end of the period we are now considering.

* Crystal balls have been frequently met with in Roman and Anglo-Saxon cemeteries in England, in France (Childeric's tomb), and in Western Germany. They are sometimes set in two rings (Akerman's 'Archæological Index,' p. 143), evidently to be suspended on the person as an ornament ('Inventorium Sepulchrale,' p. 43). Hitherto, I believe, no inscriptions had been found on them.

† A somewhat similar discovery, from Sarr, in Kent, is described in 'Archæologia Cantiana,' vol. v., 1864, by Mr. J. Brent.

B.

*Earth-finds.* Discoveries of similar objects in the earth, not associated with remains of the dead, but deposited or lost, are frequent. More than one hundred instances of this kind in our country have come to our knowledge, and very many objects have disappeared in the melting-pot and in other ways. The articles are mostly found in gravel mounds, where also graves are frequent, and many of them probably near skeletons, though, on account of the wide-spread fear amongst the labourers of mentioning the discovery of human bones, even in barrows, this point cannot be satisfactorily ascertained.

On the other hand, there are instances in which the whole arrangement plainly shows that the articles have been deposited intentionally, and many a hill evidently served as a hiding-place for treasure. Objects of value were also sometimes hidden in the level country under large stones, and now and then deposited in some piece of home-made pottery. Lastly, discoveries are often made of single objects which may have been accidentally lost.

The antiquities obtained in this manner resemble those discovered in burial-places

Bronze Vase, from Mollerup. ¼.

in all essential points. Vessels of manifold uses, and various forms and materials, are frequent. These consist of large vessels and bowls for culinary purposes, saucepans and strainers—of bronze,—vases, cups, a drinking-horn of glass, brass mountings for drinking-horns; a great variety of earthen vessels (very few of which, however, from the shattered condition in which they are generally found, have been preserved), and costly silver goblets overlaid with gold plates, on which are embossed figures. The Roman origin of many of these vessels is undoubted; many also are of Gothic workmanship, as for instance, a little bronze vase from Mollerup, in Jutland (No. 16 on the map, see the subjoined figure) and the silver goblet from Himlingöie (figured in Worsaae's Ant. no. 314), with barbarous representations of a human figure in a sitting posture, with a poniard in its hand, and some animals. The same representation is repeated three times round the upper part of the goblet. We may also mention the celebrated golden horns from Gallehuus in Slesvig,[*] with barbarous representations of men and animals; one of these had a Runic inscription, which, according to the latest interpretation of Professor P. G. Thorsen[†] is as follows:—I, Hleva, made (caused to be made) the horns for the guests, the forestmen. (EKHLEVAGASTIM: HOLTINGAM: HORNA: TAVIDO.) Many specimens of vessels are shown in Worsaae's Ant. pp. 71 to 78.

[*] They were stolen at the beginning of this century and melted down.
[†] 'The Runic Monuments of Slesvig.' Copenhagen, 1864.

Of frequent occurrence also are beads made of bronze, silver, or golden wire twisted in spirals; of glass, amber, vitrified pastes, agate and other materials (*ibid.* 369 and 376).

Pins and other ornaments for the hair sometimes occur in precious metals. Various forms are figured in Worsaae's Ant. 306, 371–373. Hanging ornaments for the ear, and other pendants, are not unfrequent (*ibid.* 375 and 377).

Finger-rings are found partly made in spirals, partly like those represented in Worsaae's Ant. nos. 382 and 383. They are mostly in gold; one specimen is known in bronze, set with a brass coin, bearing the inscription, DIVO TRAIANO PARTH. AVG. PATRI, and on the reverse a bird without legend. The type is unknown in brass, but occurs in gold (Cohen, no. 294).

Roman metal mirrors have been discovered only in two graves; one is figured in Worsaae's Ant. no. 370, the rim is pierced with holes. Combs also are rare; they are usually of bone,—in one case, of iron.

Fibulæ and brooches appear to have been very common ornaments at that period. They are of bow-shaped or circular forms, and made of various metals. Those of the pattern figured in Worsaae's Ant. nos. 388 and 389, are probably Roman; others like nos. 390 and 395, may belong to the people of the invasion. One fibula has a Runic inscription, which Professor G. Stephens reads HÆRIS O(wns). (*Ibid.* no. 384.)*

A waistband of gold (*ibid.* no. 453) is unique among these objects. It has been conjectured that it once ornamented an idol, and such may very likely have been its use.

In only one of these deposits do we find draughtsmen; seven pieces in glass and porcelain were discovered and preserved.

Weapons occur so very rarely, that but for our great depositories, the peat-mosses, we should be left almost in the dark as regards their details. The few objects obtained from earth-finds resemble those from the peat-bogs.

Almost equally scarce are horse-trappings and riding-gear; some bridle-bits in bronze and in iron (*ibid.* nos. 354 and 355); some bronze and silver pendants like those figured in this work, Thorsbjerg, Plate 15, and some spurs, are all that have been preserved or made known. The spurs of this period—the oldest known—are of two varieties. Compare the figure on p. 12, with the annexed figure (from Vimose, in Fyen); see also Worsaae's Ant. no. 486.

Iron Spur, from Vimose. ½.

Two iron axes, some fragments of knives, and some pairs of shears, of the form figured in Worsaae's Ant. nos. 362 and 363, are the only implements derived from these sources.

* The central part of this piece is not complete; judging from a similar but perfect specimen, an oval and probably ornamental plate is wanting in the middle.

Small bronze figures have been occasionally discovered. In a meadow in North Slesvig, for instance, a hollow bronze bust of Jupiter was found, of the time of the later Emperors, about five inches high. (Slesvig, No. 12 on the map.)

Occasionally these deposits are associated with Roman coins, and sometimes Roman coins are found alone. But however found, they are invariably of the first two centuries of our era, and the beginning of the third. All the Emperors between Nero and Maximus are represented, but the Antonines appear to be of most frequent occurrence.

A short account of some discoveries of this class may not be unwelcome.

### 1.

We may mention first that of Nörre Broby, near Odense, in Fyen (No. 26 on the map). In a natural elevation of the soil some labourers, digging for gravel, came upon a heap of about three cart-loads of small stones. On removing these, the following objects were brought to light:—

A large bronze cup, a little more than fifteen inches in diameter; the handle terminating in animals' heads. (Worsaae's Ant. no. 301.)

A bronze saucepan, of Roman workmanship, evidently turned on a lathe; the inner side is lined with zinc; when found, it had a wooden cover, and contained a piece of woollen cloth, about nine inches square. (*Ibid.* 309.)

Fragment of the handle of another bronze vessel, bearing a sunk stamp with raised letters DISⲚCVS F. (*Ibid.* 308.)

The mountings of a bucket; the bucket itself is lost; it stood between two stones, each about two feet long and one foot broad; these, it was reported, were the only large stones in the heap.

A richly decorated hair-pin, with golden head, and two simpler pins. (*Ibid.* 372.)

A pendant of gold, for an ear-ring? (*Ibid.* 377.)

Nine beads of thin golden plates, seven of greenish and brown transparent glass. (*Ibid.* 376.)

A bronze bridle-bit. (*Ibid.* 355.)

Two objects in bronze of the same shape, and evidently destined for the same use, as that in Thorsbjerg Plate 14, Fig. 23, of this work. (*Ibid.* 357.)

### 2.

In a gravel mound near Odense (Fyen, no. 13 on the map), an earthen vessel was exhumed, containing a hanging ornament for an earring, resembling Worsaae's Ant. no. 377; a bronze fibula, like *ibid.* 388; two little bronze buckles, of a shape common among the objects from the peat-deposits; and some small fragments, the use of which has not been explained.

3.

In a hill near Ekernförde, in South Slesvig (No. 28 on the map), a bronze vessel was met with, well secured with a cover, and containing a silver fibula, resembling Worsaae's Ant. no. 388. In the same hill were found two bronze spurs. (*Ibid.* no. 486.)

Though the greater part of these things are Roman, or at least of Roman workmanship, the Gothic element has many representatives. No doubt can exist as to the objects with Runic characters, for though barbarians in their contact with a more highly civilized people may sometimes have adopted their form of letters, we cannot presume that the reverse was the case. The works of art also afford good evidence. The silver goblet in Worsaae's Ant. no. 314, and the vase, no. 302, evidently belong to different nations, though both were found in the same locality, Himlingöie, near Præstö, in Sealand (map No. 45).

C.

*Deposits in peat-bogs* are not unfrequently discovered, and we have objects similar to those already mentioned from about thirty localities. The mosses, in which larger hoards, dating from the earliest period of the Iron age, have been found, lie along the east coast of Slesvig and North Jutland, from the Sli to the Sæbybæk, in Fyen and in Bornholm. There is great similarity in the character and ornamental details of the objects obtained from them. These are commonly personal ornaments, weapons, warlike accoutrements, and vessels for domestic purposes; the localities also are alike in the circumstance, probably not accidental, that they have a near access to the open sea or to watercourses flowing towards it. The places of deposit, it would almost seem, were chosen by a seafaring people.

The more important of these discoveries are the following:—

*a.* Slesvig.

1. *Thorsbjerg* moss, near Sönder Brarup, in Angel (map No. 26), is the southernmost of these ancient mosses; in a straight line it is distant from the Sli about three miles and a half, and the distance to the Oxbæk, which flows into the last-named firth, is about four hundred yards.

2. *Nydam* moss, near Öster Sottrup, in Sundeved (map No. 14), is distant less than a mile from the Als-Sound, with which it was formerly connected. The valley in which it lies reaches to the Sound, from which it is now separated by a dyke of only some three hundred years' standing.

*b.* North Jutland.

3. *Vingsted* mill-pond (map No. 36), near the Veile brook, and about six miles from the Firth of Veile, yielded:—

Several bosses and handles of shields, in iron and in bronze; one axe and some javelins and arrow-heads of iron.

Many articles belonging to harness, and

Fragments of golden bracelets, probably ring-money.

These things have been exposed to fire, so that many are much injured; originally they were as magnificently ornamented as the best from the Thorsbjerg-moss.

4. *Dallerup* lake, near Horsens (map No. 32), two miles and a half from the Firth of Horsens. Near the border of the lake a fisherman found—

Damascened iron swords and fragments of sword handles; spear- and arrow-heads of iron.

An iron bridle-bit. (Worsaae's Ant. no. 489.)

A sort of pitchfork of iron.

5. *Hedeliskær*, near Skjödstrup (map No. 21), is situated about a mile from Kalö Vig, in a deep valley surrounded by hills; here were found—

A golden finger-ring.

Four umbones and some rims of shields.

Five damascened swords.

Fourteen spear-heads, and no less than thirty-two arrow-heads. (*Ibid.* 342, *a* and *b*.)

An iron axe-blade, and

Four iron knives.

6. *Trinnemose*, in the parish of Thorslev, near Sæby (map No. 6), at a distance of about eight miles from the sea, yielded—

Brass mountings of a (wooden) scabbard; bronze buckles; and other fittings of sword-belts; and

Bronze bridles and pendants, exactly like some of those from Thorsbjerg moss. (Plate 14, Fig. 16, and Plate 15, Fig. 33–48.)

### c. Fyen.

7. *Vimose* (map No. 9), the moss of Wi, "temple" in Gothic, near the villages of Broby and Allesö, in the vicinity of Odense—or, as the place is called in Knytlinga Saga, Odinsve, that is Odin's place of sacrifice,—a mile and a half from the Stavis brook, which flows into the Firth of Odense. It is surrounded on all sides by hills; the locality, accordingly, agrees with that of the Thorsbjerg moss, as will be more fully described hereafter. During several years (since 1848) the peat-cutters continued to find antiquities here, which are now preserved in the Copenhagen museum; in 1859, systematic diggings were superintended by Mr. Herbst, one of the officers of the museum; and in July and August, 1865, the whole territory was examined under my guidance, and more than two thousand antiquities discovered. To give an idea of the importance of this large hoard, I shall briefly enumerate the objects.

A bronze ornament, in the form of an eagle's head, probably for a helmet; evidently of Roman manufacture. (Worsaae's Ant. 336.)

The larger portion of two coats of mail, of thin iron rings.

Personal ornaments and articles of the toilet, as—a silver finger-ring; fibulæ in bronze and silver (see Fig. *g*), and fragments of two others resembling Fig. 11, Plate 4, of this work; beads of glass and of porcelain; small round pendants, in silver, one of amber; many small bronze and iron ornaments shaped like buckets (Plate V., Fig. 15, 16, and Plate 18, Fig. 3); large buttons of glass and amber (Worsaae's Ant. no. 335); about fifty combs in bone (*ibid.* no. 365), on one is a Runic inscription of five letters—HFRSF; fragments of wooden draughtboards; on the one side are lozenges carved in the wood, on the other circles,—probably for different games; about a hundred draughts-men of bone and amber, between half an inch and three-quarters of an inch in diameter six dice of bone, quadrangular, or of an elongated square form (Fig. *c* and *e*).

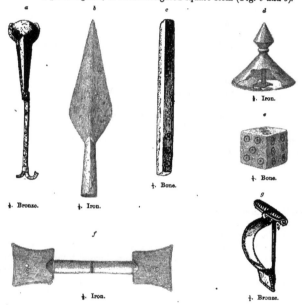

*a*

*b*

*c*

*d*

$\frac{1}{4}$. Iron.

*e*

$\frac{1}{1}$. Bone.

$\frac{1}{4}$. Bronze.

$\frac{1}{4}$. Iron.

$\frac{1}{1}$. Bone.

*g*

*f*

$\frac{1}{4}$. Iron.

$\frac{1}{4}$. Bronze.

Shields.—A great many of the boards of which they were composed, fragments of rims, bronze, iron, and silver, wooden handles, and coverings of bronze, iron, and bone; some of the latter differ considerably in shape from those obtained from the Slesvig mosses—compare the annexed chemitype, Fig. *f*,—some hundred bosses, all of iron, with the exception of a complete bronze boss, and four bosses of thick wood. Some forms were previously unknown among the umbones from the Slesvig depositories (Worsaae's Ant. 339 and 340); compare also the chemitype, Fig. *d*, of the upper part of an iron umbo.

A great variety of bronze bands for repairs; compare Plate 8, Fig. 29, of this work.

Swords, Belts, etc.—About thirty iron swords, and a great many fragments, especially of the pointed ends of the blades (Worsaae's Ant. nos. 321 to 324); only two of the blades appear to have been damascened. One-edged swords are not unfrequent, and judging from their resemblance to some Anglo-Saxon or Old English swords, they are of a comparatively late date. Just beneath the tang of one of the two-edged swords the inscription TASVIT is found in raised Roman letters. A two-edged wooden sword, many fragments of sword-handles of ivory (*ibid.* 325 and 326), and about fifty in wood, compare Plate 9, Fig. 2, of this work. A few complete scabbards of wood, and about two hundred mountings in silver, bronze, iron, and brass, of (wooden) scabbards (Worsaae's Ant. 331 and 332); one has an inscription of four Runic characters (*ibid.* 331); others the fylfot ornament. That the embossed central part of the mountings, shaped like no. 332, is meant for an imitation of a bird's head, is clearly proved by the annexed chemitype, Fig. *a*, of a specimen from this locality, in which the eyes are represented by blue paste. (From a private collection.)

About a hundred and fifty chapes, or scabbard-tips, fifteen in ivory, a few in bone, the majority of bronze (*ibid.* 328, 329, and 333; the last is drawn in an inverted position, it is made of silver, and covered with a thin gold plate, on which a human head is embossed; the workmanship is evidently barbarous and late).

Two leather belts and about fifty large belt-buttons, of a shape like that figured in Plate 11, Fig. 48 *a* and 48 *b*, of this work; four of these exhibit one and the same representation on a thin gold plate, covering the centre of the surface, viz. the eagle with the fulmen in his claws and a ring in his bill, on both sides trophies; all of Roman workmanship. A great many buckles in silver, bronze, and iron.

Spear-heads.—About fifteen hundred iron heads of lances and missiles, partly resembling some from Nydam moss (Plates 10 and 11); partly of other forms (Worsaae's Ant. 344 to 352). None of the lances have had a spike at foot, but the end of the shaft is rounded. (No. 345, in Worsaae, is drawn in an inverted position, the original being in reality a fragment of a socketed spear-head.) On many, ornaments are inlaid in silver and gold. (*Ibid.* no. 347.) Others are ornamented like Figs. 8 and 9 on Plate X., from Nydam. Some forms resembling those from the old English graves, indicate a somewhat later date for the whole deposit than that of the two Slesvig deposits.

Wooden shafts in great abundance; the complete shafts were from nine feet four inches to eleven feet four inches long; many of them with bronze rivets.

Bows, Arrows, Quiver, Sharpening-stones.—Some wooden bows and many fragments, about a hundred arrow-heads of bone and iron. Worsaae's Ant. no. 341 *a, b,* and *c,* are instances of the arrow-heads. Fragment of a large wooden quiver. A great many sharpening-stones. (*Ibid.* 343.)

Horse-trappings and Riding-gear.—Fragment of a bronze bridle, resembling that figured in Plate 14, Fig. 21, iron bits, and about one hundred pendants, resembling those figured in Plate 15. Fig. 33–48. Spurs of the different forms which were in use during this period. (See pages 12 and 15.)

Household Vessels, Implements, Tools, etc.—Fragments of a large wooden (water) trough, in its perfect state probably, something like the original of that represented in Plate XIV. Fig. 25, and smaller domestic vessels of burnt clay and of wood. The former are hand-made; the latter elaborately turned on a lathe, and some of their handles cut into shapes of griffins, dragons, lizards, crocodiles, etc. A wooden spoon, with a long magnificently ornamented handle.

About a hundred iron knives, some with handles of wood and bone. (Worsaae's Ant. no. 360 and 361.) Fragments of a pair of shears, like Worsaae's Ant. no. 363.

Handles of awls of wood and bone.

About forty iron axes of the two different forms belonging to this period; the varieties are seen in Plate XV. Nydam, Fig. 10 and 13; the wooden shafts of the latter specimens were here shorter and of another form.

Complete files, hammers, chamfering planes—one of which has inscriptions upon it consisting of forty-four Runic characters,—gimlets, tongs, chisels, and other tools, all in iron, with wooden shafts; a little anvil of the same substance; iron moulds in which small buttons have been cast, etc. Some pierced touchstones, shafts of bones (Worsaae's Ant. no. 358), small rough pieces of amber, cords made of bast, a bronze key, bronze scales, very like the ordinary form of the present day, etc.

A silver coin of Faustina Junior.

A little boat, about ten feet long, hollowed out of an oak trunk;* some small oars. Fragments of wooden wheels, and some fragments of wooden rakes (?).

Two small chopping-blocks of oak. In their vicinity, as well as almost everywhere else in the layer of antiquities, a great many bones of animals, especially of horses, were taken up. Many of these bones were chopped and splintered, and bore evident marks of man's handiwork.

Characteristic of this hoard are the numerous objects of ivory, a substance which has been found in none of the other Danish peat-bogs, the many tools, and to some extent also the many bones of animals, found among the other objects, and evidently deposited together with them. Many objects bear traces of fire upon them.

The peculiarities of this locality are exactly the same as those I have observed in the two peat-bogs before described.

* Vimose is surrounded by hills, and has probably never been in direct connection with the sea, so that we cannot expect to find such large boats there as those from Nydam.

8. *Villestofte* moss, near Paarup (map No. 11), lies close to the Stavis brook, in the direct line to the Firth of Odense, about five miles distant. A chape of bone, several mountings for wooden scabbards, and a bone comb, were here dug up by peat-cutters. No systematic diggings have taken place.

9. *Kragehul* (map No. 22), a little moss near the village of Flemlöse, about four miles from the Little Belt. The antiquities found here were: two-edged damascened iron swords with handles of silver and bronze; metal mountings appertaining to wooden sheaths, chapes of bronze, etc. (some of them arranged together in Worsaae's Ant. no. 330); iron spear-heads, and very richly and finely ornamented shafts;

 several bows of wood, and arrow-heads of iron and bone (*ibid.* 353 *a* and *b*); many iron knives (*ibid.* 359); two camp-kettles of bronze, bent up and mutilated, wooden vessels; a fragment of wood, probably forming part of some handle, with Runic inscription (see the annexed figure), etc.

### d. Bornholm.

10. In Römmere moss (map No. 1) were dug up—a bent iron sword, chape, and several sheath-mountings; bronze rims of shields; two bronze vessels (camp-kettles), similar to those found in Kragehul and to that in Neville's 'Saxon Obsequies,' plate xvi.; they are bent and mutilated in a curious manner.

These objects, it is reported, were in such a condition that they had obviously been unfit for use at the time of their being deposited.

No doubt can exist as to the objects found in these different localities—graves, mosses, etc.—belonging to one and the same period or stage of civilization; but further and more systematic investigations, particularly of the graves, are necessary in order to solve all questions of detail. When these investigations have been carried out, we shall better understand the character of the moss deposits, and we shall be enabled to distinguish with greater confidence between the Roman, semi-Roman, and Barbarian relics belonging to this age; only then can we attempt to fix with accuracy the beginning of the Iron age in the North as well as in the West of Europe.

23

# CHAPTER II.

## LOCAL PECULIARITIES OF THORSBJERG AND NYDAM.

THE name of Thorsbjerg, which signifies the Hill of Thor, appears inappropriate for a peat-moss, nor is it in truth originally the name of the moss, but of an enclosure on the adjacent hills. It lies north of the village of Sönder Brarup, in Angel, and is surrounded on all sides by sand-hills. Within a distance of about four hundred yards, there is a brook, named the Oxbæk, which rises in the vicinity, and flowing southward, falls into the Sli (D on the accompanying map). This brook may possibly have been navigable in ancient times; and though the moss is now surrounded on all sides by hills, and has no outlet for its waters, the sand-hills may possibly be of comparatively recent origin; and even if the brook were not navigable at the time when the objects were deposited, there was a ready access from the moss to the sea; the Firth of Sli being only about three miles distant, in a direct line southwards. I make this remark in order to draw attention to the resemblance between this and other Danish mosses, which have yielded discoveries of this kind, all of which lie in the vicinity of rivers or streams affording easy

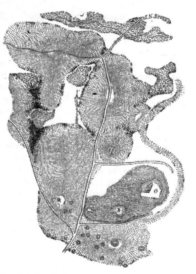

communication with the sea. (See the map of Denmark, facing page 8, and the preceding chapter.)

This little moss has a very inviting appearance to the eye of the antiquary. On the adjacent hill to the south, there are no less than sixteen barrows of various sizes. Some of these were opened in the hope that antiquities of the same age as those in the moss might be discovered in them; but they were found to belong to the Bronze period.*

The bottom of the valley, the lower part of which has been filled up by the peat, is very irregular. The hills and sloping grounds of the immediate vicinity are here found upon the whole on a smaller scale, yet forming among other irregularities two larger dips, marked A and B on the annexed map. In the easternmost of these dips the antiquities in question were found scattered over the space of about eight thousand square feet, comprised within the lines round the letter O. The majority of them were in the centre of this space, their number decreasing towards the circumference.

The section observed in the moss is shown in the annexed woodcut, where *a* and *b*

represent a layer of peat about eleven feet in thickness. The deeper we go down, the closer and more compressed does the peat appear. In the lowest part of this layer, some ten feet under the present surface, were found some lighter objects, garments, boards of shields, articles of leather and basket-work. We may safely suppose that these floated on the water at the time when the objects were sunk into what was then a lake bordered with trees. The appearance of the upper sides of the wooden objects which were met with at this depth, confirms this opinion; they bear traces of long exposure to the air, and have a dark colour. The under side, on the contrary, is quite smooth, and light in colour, as are the wooden objects found in the next layer (*c*), which look as if they had been finished yesterday.

This next layer, *c* on the woodcut, contained, with the exception of the few articles mentioned above, all the objects found. It is about five feet thick, and consists of the soft and dark, almost black substance, from which peat is cut for fuel. The line *l* marks the depth at which trunks of beech-trees, once growing at the sides of the lake, are found close up to the hillsides; the line *n* shows where the fir trunks commence. There is much reason to suppose, from the relative position of these trunks, that a fir wood bordered the lake at the time when these articles were submerged.

Beneath this there is a layer about twelve feet thick, consisting chiefly of leaves of forest-trees and water-plants, a substance unfit for fuel. The conditions necessary for the growth of peat may not have existed at the time when these leaves and plants were exposed to the air, and afterwards they were closely shut out from atmospheric action by the layers gradually formed over them.

* Notice of two barrows of the Bronze age in 'Slesvigske Provindsial-Efterretninger' (October, 1863).

The bottom of the peat-bog consists of white sand, with many small white shells on the surface.

Though peat has been cut to a considerable depth over almost the whole moss, no antiquities have appeared outside.the space marked *o*.  It is therefore more than probable that the systematic diggings which, with the liberal and ever-ready assistance of the Danish Government, were carried on during certain periods of the summers of 1858 to 1861, have brought to light the entire deposit.  There is, moreover, no doubt that what has now been dug up was all deposited at about the same time, as a thick layer of vegetable matter had in course of time accumulated, covering the stratum which contained the antiquities, and thus affording a security against any extraneous object finding its way into the original deposit.

If we now turn our attention to the circumstances under which the objects were originally deposited, and their condition when discovered, we cannot but notice the remarkable fact that a certain order in the mode of deposit is plainly observable. Not only were wooden articles often lying in large heaps,—as, for instance, several layers of shields one above the other, occasionally also with javelins stuck through them to keep them together,—but certain classes of objects were almost all found together in one place.  This was, for instance, the case with nearly all objects of gold, and one particular spot the workmen called " chain-mail close," knowing that we should probably find some of these articles there.   The vessels of burnt clay, having been sunk by placing large stones in them, lay at the greatest depth ; and sometimes spear-heads and smaller arms were wrapped up in coats of mail.  These are a few examples out of many, but they go far, I think, to prove that the whole was purposely sunk in the water, and that this and similar accumulations of antiquities cannot be considered accidental, or explained by supposing that a great number of warriors have fallen through the ice during a battle in winter, or on any similar hypothesis.  Moreover, human remains have never been found during the systematic exploration of the two Slesvig mosses.

Another noteworthy circumstance is that most of the objects found are in such a condition that they must have been unfit for use when they were deposited.  All the umbones, with scarcely one exception, are bent and crumpled, or pierced by javelins and arrow-heads in a manner which cannot be explained as the result of even a desperate struggle.  This has evidently been done on purpose.  One sheath was cut in two, and many wooden sheaths were deprived of their mountings and fittings of metal. Bridles consisting of solid metal rings, are cut and injured in many places, and costly metal plates have been torn off, apparently in a hurried manner, from the objects which they decorated.

One circumstance serves to a certain degree to explain the incomplete condition of many of the articles brought to light on this occasion.  Iron is almost entirely consumed by the water of this peat-bog.  In many places, vestiges of corroded iron were

E

seen in the black peat, indicating that iron articles had been thrown in along with the others, but only very small fragments of iron objects had been preserved, and these were almost exclusively found in the upper layer, about a foot above the other remains. It is fortunate that the tannic acid of the Nydam moss has not this corrosive quality in the same degree as that of the Thorsbjerg moss. Numbers of iron weapons and implements of about the same period have been preserved in Nydam, and this deposit, in connection with that of Thorsbjerg, presents a vivid picture of the civilization of the Early Iron period, in so far as it may be inferred from remains of dress, weapons, household utensils, horse furniture, and ship building.

It is further to be remarked that some of these relics had been exposed to fire, traces of which were discovered on objects of wood and metal, as well as on some of the coins. Pieces of charcoal were of frequent occurrence, they were even now and then found in small heaps. The traces of old repairs and patchings are frequent on bows and arrows, shields and bosses. Many no doubt are repairs of injuries received in combat.

*Nydam* moss lies a little towards the north-west of the school of Öster Sottrup, in

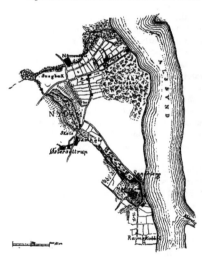

Sundeved, scarcely fourteen hundred yards from the Als Sound. The narrow valley, of which it fills the bottom, is about two miles long, and stretches, as will be seen from the annexed map,[*] in the direction of north-west to south-east to the Sound. The dams, which now separate the inner part, where the antiquities have been discovered, from Damhale and the mill-pond, and this again from the Sound, date back to the year 1579. Nydam[†] was accordingly in olden time part of an arm of the sea, and it was navigable at the time when the objects of which we treat were deposited,—a fact which may also be inferred from the boats found there.

The antiquities were deposited on the sandy and clayey bottom, at a depth of between four and seven feet.

The diggings made during the summers of 1859, 1862, and 1863, led to about the same results with regard to the manner in which the objects had been deposited, and the state they were in, as the exploration of Thorsbjerg-moss.

[*] 1000 Danish ells are equal to about 2060 English feet.     [†] The word signifies "The New Pond."

The antiquities were found scattered over a space of ten thousand square feet, in many cases collected into heaps, and tied together or wrapped up in linen. Such parcels were, for instance, found in the different compartments of the boat between the ribs, and bundles of twenty or thirty arrows were not unfrequent. Some of the spears and swords had been planted perpendicularly, their points reaching as much as three or four feet deeper than the ordinary stratum of antiquities. As in the Thorsbjerg-moss, only very few of the articles had been in a perfect and serviceable state at the time of their deposit; almost all had been much injured, as may be seen, for instance, from some of the handles on Plate VI., and many chapes on Plate IX.; swords and spearheads had been cut and bent in a curious manner, barbs were wrenched out of their original position (Plate XI.); staves had in many instances been cut in two and split, etc. etc.

It seems hardly possible to explain all these traces of violence as the effects of a conflict. One sword-blade (Plate VII.) shows no less than twenty-three marks on one edge and eleven on the other, which appear to have been purposely caused, and almost everything exhibits traces of such violent handling. Not even the skeletons of horses have been spared. One of the heads had thirteen marks of blows (see the annexed figure) inflicted with a sharp instrument, probably a sword.

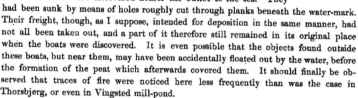

I believe all the objects found in this locality to have lain originally in the boats, of which so many remains were discovered. Where the antiquities lay thickest, and among them, were discovered planks of a very elegant oak-built boat, cut asunder and completely destroyed. This boat it would appear, from its relative position to the other boats, had first come into the creek,—its remains were found in the innermost recess of it; the cargo had been taken out and deposited in the water in precisely the same manner as was observed in Thorsbjerg. The two other boats were discovered nearer the outlet to the sea. They had been sunk by means of holes roughly cut through planks beneath the water-mark. Their freight, though, as I suppose, intended for deposition in the same manner, had not all been taken out, and a part of it therefore still remained in its original place when the boats were discovered. It is even possible that the objects found outside these boats, but near them, may have been accidentally floated out by the water, before the formation of the peat which afterwards covered them. It should finally be observed that traces of fire were noticed here less frequently than was the case in Thorsbjerg, or even in Vingsted mill-pond.

The common origin of all the deposits of this kind discovered in our peat-bogs is obvious, and it is further evident, that for the most part they have been made under similar circumstances and for the same reasons. When attempting to answer the question why so many objects, which even in their mutilated state must have been of

great value to their former owners, were sunk in what were then lakes, we must not
lose sight of the following facts, namely,—that many were placed in a certain order;
that most of them were in a condition unfit for *immediate* use; that they bear marks of
having been almost all *intentionally* spoiled or injured; and that there is in many instances evidence of their having been in some cases exposed to fire.  The suggestion of
a German *savant* that these relics may indicate the sites of ancient lake-dwellings is
inadmissible, as the piles characteristic of such spots are entirely absent.  More probable is the hypothesis of M. Beauvois, a French author, who has spent some time in
Denmark, and has published an interesting account of Danish antiquities in the 'Revue
Contemporaine,' 1863 and 1864.  He suggests that these bogs may have been a kind
of lacustrine cemeteries in which the dead were buried with arms and other accessories,
as is still the case with some modern savages.*  In support of his theory he adduces
several arguments from Northern Mythology, as well as the fact that objects found in
the graves are often similarly mutilated, but there is this strong objection, that hardly
any human remains have been found in these mosses, and many of the objects are such
as could hardly have been deposited with the dead.  Mr. J. J. A. Worsaae† has lately
suggested that these peat-mosses may have been in ancient times sacred lakes, in which
these objects were deposited as offerings, such a custom having prevailed among the Gauls
and other nations during the first centuries of our era.‡  According to Mr. Worsaae,
this hypothesis would account for the traces of sharp weapons, as many of the objects
may have been picked up on fields of battle; it would perhaps account for the traces
of fire, for the chopping-blocks and the bones of horses and other animals dispersed
among the antiquities of Vimose, supposing them to be the remains from sacrificial
meals.  But it does not explain satisfactorily the intentionally mutilated state of many,
nay, most of the objects.

We regret that we are unable at present satisfactorily to solve these enigmas.  We
may, however, add, that systematic explorations have as yet been undertaken in only
four of these interesting hiding-places—the two Slesvig mosses and the two mosses in
Fyen.  Undoubtedly, the receptacles of many large hoards are yet unexplored, and
further researches can scarcely fail to throw much new light on the subject.

* Lubbock's Prehistoric Times, p. 455.  Compare also Mr. Kanes's remarkable account in the ' Cana-
dian Journal,' Jan. 1857, p. 22, of the customs of the Chinook Indians at the mouth of the Columbia river,
who deposit their dead in canoes, together with arms, paddles, and other implements, food and ornaments,
and even coin.  The canoes are fixed in trees or placed near the ground, in certain islands serving as cemeteries, and every article left with the body is *rendered entirely useless*, their belief being that the Great
Spirit will mend it on the deceased arriving at the hunting-ground of their Elysium.  The greatest crime
an Indian could commit would be that of desecrating one of these canoes, and it very seldom happens that
the smallest thing is removed.

† ' Om Slesvigs eller Sönderjyllands Oldtidsminder,' Copenhagen, 1865, pp. 55–59.

‡ Mr. Worsaae refers to Cæsar, De Bello Gallico, vi. 16, 17; Strabo, Geogr. iv. 1813; Gregorius
Turonensis, De Gloriâ Confess. ch. ii. (Maxima Bibl. Patrum, xi. 872); Diodorus Siculus, v. 27.  Compare
also Sir J. Lubbock, Prehist. Times, 160, where several other references will be found.

# CHAPTER III.

## DESCRIPTION OF THE OBJECTS FOUND.

### 1. BOATS.

#### (Nydam, Plates I.–IV.)

THE three rowing-boats discovered in Nydam-moss are unique of their kind, and will, perhaps, remain so for a long time to come. They throw an entirely new light on the naval architecture of ancient times, and are indeed among the most important results of the antiquarian investigations of our peat-mosses. As early as the summer of 1859, part of an oar was found, being the first naval relic of the Early Iron age ever discovered, and the remaining part of the same oar was found in 1862. On the 7th of August, 1863, the remains of the first boat (Plate IV. Fig. 27) were found on the spot marked A in the map (p. 26); and on the 18th of the same month, the large and magnificent oak-built boat, represented from different points of view on Plate I. Fig. 1, 2, was discovered lying in the direction of south-east to north-west, the main direction of the valley, leaning over on the north-eastern side, and, as was clearly shown by holes cut in the planks under water-mark, intentionally sunk. Later in the same autumn, the third boat, which was built of fir, was found at the side of the oak boat, and parallel with it; and on the 27th of October, 1863, it was laid bare in the presence of King Frederick VII., and afterwards taken up.

The first of these boats had, at the time when these deposits were formed, been so completely destroyed, that only fragments were found, and the state of these fragments throws much light over the whole matter, because the destruction was so evidently intentional. The fragments, viz. planks with projecting ornamented clamps, and row-locks but little different in shape from those belonging to the other boats, sufficiently prove that the construction of all the boats was essentially the same.

It is to the second boat that we must principally direct our attention, because it was not only the best preserved of the three, so as to allow of reconstruction, but fortunately for the interests of science, Mr. Stephensen, of Copenhagen, restorer of antiquities, to whom the work was entrusted, succeeded in almost completing its restoration before the commencement of the war in 1864. These investigations were then interrupted, and the objects discovered scattered, the greater part being in all probability now lost.*

When first discovered, the boat was of course no longer in its original state. In course of time the washers of the bolts by which the planks were fastened together had corroded, the ropes joining the outer parts of the boat to the inner framework had been destroyed, the planks in consequence had separated and reassumed their original shape, the rowlocks had fallen from the gunwale, the ribs had sunk out of their proper places, and lay in different directions, whilst the stem and stern-posts had detached themselves from the bottom plank. By degrees, as the boat fell to pieces, these sank to the bottom to about the same depth, whilst the peat, at the same time, grew up around them, covering and protecting them from destruction. The shape of the boat could not therefore be directly ascertained from the pieces found, and the sketches of it given on Plate I. Fig. 1 and 2, were not made until, after the lapse of so many centuries, it had been restored to its original form in the Museum of Northern Antiquities at Flensborg. No drawing, however, can fully convey the striking impression produced by the large, sharp, and well-built boat itself.

The boat is seventy-seven feet long, measured from stem to stern, and proportionally rather broad in the middle, viz. ten feet ten inches, flat at the bottom, but higher and sharper at each end ; it consists of eleven oak-planks, viz. five on either side, besides the bottom plank, of which the keel forms part, the latter being only a little more than one inch deep and fully eight inches broad at the middle of the boat, gradually diminishing and at last vanishing entirely towards the stem-posts (Plate II. Fig. 4 and 5).

On all the planks there are perforated clamps of one and the same piece with the planks themselves, having been left projecting when the planks were cut out of the solid timber,—a most surprising fact, considering the high development to which the smith's art had been carried by the people of the Early Iron period ; a fact too, which proves

* The original intention was to form all the remains of boats and what belonged to them found at Nydam into a separate naval division of the Museum of Northern Antiquities at Flensborg. The building where the museum was, contained several lofts under its high roof, and in one of these the remains of the oak boat were brought and put together, filling the middle of the room, whilst oars, etc., would have been arranged along the walls. But the war put an end to all this, as not only the supply of money ceased with the authority of the Danish Government, by whose liberality the museum had been founded, and the systematic investigations carried on ; but, moreover, the confusion consequent on the foreign occupation rendered such work impossible, and I, myself, was soon compelled to leave the town. The chief part of the collection had fortunately been removed previous to the invasion ; but the boat is, of course, still in its place, and a friend who obtained a view of it when at Flensborg last autumn, states that it appeared not much the worse, which, perhaps, may be ascribed to the circumstance, that many pieces of the old timber, particularly of the ribs, were found too weak to bear the strain of the new bolts, and therefore had to be replaced by exact copies of fresh timber, made under my own superintendence. Of course, all the descriptions and measures given above, are taken from the originals.

that they must have possessed a great abundance of timber, as they would not otherwise have wasted it to that degree, only in order to save a few nails, or to secure the clamps so much better.

The boat is clinker-built; the planks held together by large iron nails, at intervals of five inches and a half, with large rounded heads outside, and square burrs or washers inside (Plate III. Fig. 13). The spaces between the planks where they lap over one another were filled up—caulked—with woollen stuff and a pitchy sticky substance. The planks are cut from very fine pieces of timber; the bottom plank being forty-six feet eight inches long, and all of one piece. On both stems, which are fixed to the bottom plank by means of wooden pegs (Plate II. Fig. 8), there are ornamental grooves, and each of them shows two large holes, which, to judge from the marks of wear, most likely have served to pass the ropes through, when the boat was to be hauled on shore. The ribs, which give the boat its shape, are mostly in their natural crooked and irregularly bent shape, and rest on the clamps projecting from the planks, which form regular rows across the boat, those on one plank exactly corresponding to those on the next. The ribs have perforations corresponding to the clamps, through which bast ropes were passed, tying planks and ribs together (Plate II. Fig. 2–5). This is again a fact highly surprising in a nation familiar with the use of iron, and able to work it so well, as their damascened swords prove that they could. At the same time, it is possible that a loose connection between the framework and the planking of the boat served to give more elasticity to the sides, and that boats built in this manner went through the surf and great waves easier than those more strongly built.

The shape of the gunwale will be understood from Fig. 5 *a* in Plate II.; on it were fixed the rowlocks, which, although made on the same general model, yet all differed from one another in size or in the details of the work. Fig. 15–18 on Plate III. represent some of the best preserved. They were tied to the gunwale by means of bast ropes, and in this case too it might seem surprising that for the fixing of such important pieces as the rowlocks, recourse should have been had to such weak fastenings, which must so often have required to be renewed. But this method had at the same time the advantage of rendering it possible to turn them, when necessary, and row the boat in the opposite direction, particularly as both ends of the boat are so exactly alike, that it is difficult to say which is the prow and which is the stern. It is true that the width of the boat at the fourth rib is a few inches greater than at the fifteenth rib, which corresponds to it at the other end; but this difference is so small, that it was probably not intentional, and the boat has no doubt been designed to shoot through the waves with equal speed, whichever way it was rowed. Its shape therefore, in some respects, reminds us of Tacitus's description of the ships of the Suiones.* For their ships differed from those of the Romans, particularly in this, that the stems were exactly alike, so that whichever way they were rowed, they had a prow fit for resisting a col-

* Germania, c. 44.

lision or for landing ; and besides, the ships of the Suiones had no sails. Tacitus further says of these boats, that their oars were not fixed in a row along the sides, but were loose, as in certain craft used on rivers, and could be put into the water on either side, as might be required ; but this part of the description would not apply to the boats found at Nydam, for on them the oars were passed through loops of rope tied to the rowlocks, on which the marks of wear by the oars are still quite visible ; they could not be turned the other way without loss of time and labour, nor would it be possible to back the oars for any length of time, or with sufficient precision, when they are thus tied to the rowlocks.

It is a remarkable and very significant fact, which has only recently come to my knowledge, that this curious kind of rowlock, so different from those now generally adopted by seafaring nations, and which evidently in ancient times was used in this the southernmost part of the Scandinavian countries, is still in use in their northernmost provinces, viz. along the coast of Norway, from Egersund or Lister round the North Cape to the frontiers of Russia, a distance of twelve hundred geographical miles. The boats used on this coast, called " Nordlandsbaade," Northland boats, remind us, in many respects, of those discovered in Nydam. They are described as long, narrow and low, light and elegant, fit both for rowing and sailing. I have had no opportunity of seeing these boats myself, but, to judge from drawings of them, their outward appearance is surprisingly like the Nydam boats. Only it seems as if these latter were proportionally still longer and narrower, and consequently sharper, than the Northland boats, as may be seen from the following comparative table of measures :—

> A Northland boat may be . 42 feet long, 10 feet broad, with 16 oars.
> The large boat from Nydam is 77  „  10½  „  with 28 oars.

A still closer approach to the dimensions of the Nydam boat is afforded by the river-boats of the Norwegian Finns, which are longer, narrower, and flatter than the Northland boats.

One of the Norwegian authors, from whose papers in " Folkevennen " of 1863 and 1865 these details are borrowed,—Mr. Diriks and Mr. E. Sundt,—states that " the Northland boat, such as it is now and probably has been for centuries, affords a model of those clippers, which of late years have traversed the great oceans with such astonishing speed, and probably are among the most excellent products of modern naval architecture." I have no doubt but that the boats from Nydam present us with at least one of the models for the Northland boats, which on the occasion of the great herring and cod fisheries on the coasts of Norway assemble to the number of ten thousand on the Norwegian coast. For not only do they agree in the general form, but also in this,— that the planks of the Northland boats are held together by clincher nails, in the same way as the Nydam boats (whilst in more southern countries the boat-planks are now-adays joined by wooden pegs), and more surprisingly still, in the peculiar construction of the rowlocks. It is therefore probable that this form of boat dates from a very remote period when the "iron people" invaded Norway from the South and East (Denmark and Sweden) and brought it with them from their former home. Mr. Diriks says, "During the last century no change has taken place with regard to these boats in Norway, for in some places in the Northlands, boats are met with, more than a hundred years old, which are not different from those built nowadays. A kind of Northland boat is also still in use in the Shetland Islands—one of the ancient appurtenances of the Norwegian Crown. As for the rowlocks of the Northland boats, their shape may be understood from the annexed figure, representing one of them taken from a new boat built at Ranenfjord in the "Nordlands Amt," about lat. 66° N. They are called "Keiper," and the same term (Keipr) is found in old Icelandic Sagas (Fornmanna Sögur), and in Snorro's Edda, and is translated "scalmus navigii." The "Keiper" consist of a piece of wood fastened to the gunwale by wooden pegs, bearing an oblique prolongation at one end, and furnished with

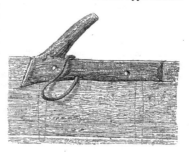

a loop of wicker-work, rope, or leather, through which the oar is passed, and which prevents its slipping out of the Keip while rowing. These rowlocks, which evidently are of the same kind as those on the Nydam boats, are in Norway considered superior to the ordinary tholes, being not so liable to break as the latter.

At the side of the oak boat, about ten feet distant from the stem, the *rudder* was discovered (Plate II. Fig. 9). Its length is nine feet seven inches, and near the middle it has a hole, through which a rope may have been passed for the purpose of tying it to the side of the boat; just below this hole there is a little cushion of wood fixed with three wooden pegs, intended to protect the rudder from injury by knocking or grating against the side of the boat, and at the top end there is a loose piece with two handles.

This is the most ancient form of rudder known. Rudders quite similar to this in shape and construction may be seen on many representations of the ships of classic times, and always on the right-hand, "starboard," of the steersman. Lateral rudders were retained down to a rather late period, and are represented, for instance, on the Bayeux tapestry (the middle of the eleventh century), in the bas-reliefs over the door of the Leaning Tower at Pisa, built in the twelfth century, and on the seal of the town of Sandwich on a document of 1238. This kind of rudder must have been in use even after the middle of the thirteenth century, for in contracts concerning ships to be built

F

for Louis XI., the builders promise to furnish them with two rudders. It was only at the close of the thirteenth century that the side rudder was supplanted by the hinged rudder now in use.*

In Fig. 6, Plate II., and 29, Plate IV., I have tried to represent how the thwarts were constructed, strengthened by two angular boards underneath, and supported by three perpendicular pieces of wood. Only in one place, by the middle thwart, these boards were tolerably well preserved; but even there the ends were so soft as not to admit of any very complete examination, and it remains uncertain in what way they were fixed to the sides of the boat. A wicker-work mat covered the bottom of the boat.

*Oars* were found in several places outside the boat. Their size and shape will be seen from Fig. 19 and 20 on Plate III. I am unable to say what the use was of the small tenon projecting from the end of the blade of one of these oars.

Nor can I give any further information concerning the large iron anchor, of the same shape and construction as those now in use, which is reported to have been found in the excavations instituted on the 8th of August, 1864, by Prince Ahrenberg, in the Austrian service, and which may have belonged to one of the boats.

For further details concerning the structure of the boat and what belonged to it, externally and internally, I beg to refer to the four first plates, and the explanation of them at the end of this work.

As I have stated before, the oak boat had been intentionally sunk by means of large holes cut in one of its sides under water-mark; at the same time it had been caused to lean over on that side which was nearest the shore, that is, on the north-eastern side. Besides this, the stem-posts had in course of time detached themselves from the bottom plank, leaving a large opening at each end. All these circumstances had necessarily caused a great part of the contents of the boat to float or drift out of it. But a part remained, and showed, in several respects, an intentional arrangement, objects of the same kind being accumulated into heaps at particular places.

Besides some stones of moderate size heaped together in one of the partitions about the middle of the boat, and probably serving as ballast, the following objects were found in the oak boat:

A great number of round sticks, a little more than three feet long and one inch diameter, with a peculiar kind of perforation at the ends (Plate III. Fig. 23). They were found in heaps in the partitions between the thwarts, in one place near the middle, as many as thirty or forty together in a bundle; others quite similar were also found in the fir boat. Their use is unknown.

Large pieces of wood of another kind, forty-one to sixty-two inches long, the ends dilated, rounded and perforated (Plate IV. Fig. 26), were frequently found both inside and outside both boats, but their use is equally unknown.

* A. Jal, ' Archéologie Navale,' *passim*; Smith's ' Voyage and Shipwreck of St. Paul.'

A pair of massive roughly-cut poles, found in the oak boat, may have served for shoving the boat along. A precisely similar pair was found in the fir boat. Their length is in one case thirteen feet ten inches, and in the other twenty feet seven inches. (Plate III. Fig. 21 and 22.)

Two brooms, of thin branches tied together by means of string, and just like the modern brooms, were also found in the oak boat, but the broomsticks were not discovered.

In one partition of the boat, the principal contents were boards of shields, in another, arrows and wooden vessels; near one of the stems there were several swords, and small axes, and all the bronze fibulæ.

There were besides, discovered scattered in different parts of the boat, some glass beads, a comb of bone, an earpick and forceps on a ring, several vessels and basins of wood and clay, one clay vase containing a comb of bone; several axes, partly like the modern ones, partly like the so-called celts;[*] many knives; two shield bosses, one of which was of iron, covered with silver, which again was overlaid with gold; a single iron spear; several wooden bows; a wooden figure of a bird with one flat side (*vide* the transverse section, Plate IV. Fig. 33), which looks as if it might have served as an ornament on a boat, etc.

The objects found in the boat entirely correspond with the other objects found at Nydam.

The *fir boat* was tolerably complete when first discovered, and its different parts were brought on shore during the next following days after it had been laid bare and the contents taken out, in the presence of King Frederick VII., on the 27th of October, 1863. In order to protect the timber of this boat until the restoration of the oak boat was finished, it was covered over with peat, but before anything could be done to save it, the country was occupied by hostile armies in the spring of 1864. The foreign occupants did nothing to protect it,—a forcible proof of their want of true interest in that country of the history of which it forms so valuable an illustration! Since the Germans took possession of the Duchy, the fir boat has remained on the field, exposed alike to the destructive influence of the weather and the Vandalism of strangers. Parts of it have been carried away, and the last remnant will probably soon be destroyed and disappear.

I can only offer my readers sketches of the most remarkable parts of this boat; a representation of it in its perfect condition could only have been obtained if it had been reconstructed, or if, such as it was, it had received at the hands of the foreigners that attention and care to which, in a scientific point of view, it was so justly entitled.

The bottom plank (*vide* the chemitype overleaf) was about fifty-one feet four inches long, and ended in two points, which probably have carried long and pointed iron

---

[*] It should be observed that Danish archæologists restrict this appellation to axes and chisels with hollow sockets for the reception of the shafts.

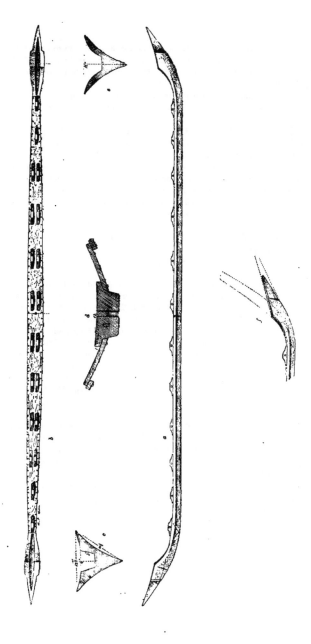

Fig. *a* represents a side view of the bottom plank of the fir boat; *b* the same piece seen from above; *c*, *d*, and *e* are transverse sections in the middle and at both ends, on a somewhat larger scale than *a* and *b*. Fig. *f* indicates by dotted lines the supposed outlines of the iron spur and the stem. The bottom plank is entirely perforated near the centre of the boat by a hole of two inches diameter.

spurs; if so, these spurs must have been under water. I cannot with certainty determine the elevation of the stems, but refer to the annexed Figure, *f.*

Of the side planks an idea may be formed from Fig. *g*; they have had clamps ornamented with mouldings, and cut out of the same piece of timber as the planks, just as in the two oak-boats. The shape of the rowlocks is somewhat different, and they have formed a continuous row along the gunwale, as indicated by Fig. 24 and 24 *a.* Plate IV. which also show the way in which each of them was joined to its neighbour.

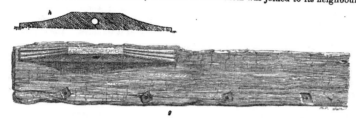

*g*

Fig. *g* represents a fragment of one of the side planks of the fir boat, with projecting clamps, and marks in the wood of the burrs of the rivets. The thickness of the planks is one inch, and the breadth between nine and ten inches. The intervals between the rivets seven inches. Fig. *h* represents a clamp viewed from the side. The clamps were fifteen inches and a half long, one inch and three-quarters high, and one inch and a quarter broad.

In this boat, as in the oak boat, the planking was tied to the ribs by ropes passing through the holes in the clamps, and the principle of the construction was the same; the great peculiarity of the fir boat being the terminal prolongations of the bottom plank, which probably have carried iron points,—a dangerous weapon of attack, equally fit for sinking an enemy's vessel, or holding it firm while being boarded. The boats provided with these spurs have been a kind of rams, and remind us of the account of the ships of the Meopari in Aithiko's 'Cosmography.'

As in the oak boat, the bottom was covered by a mat of wicker-work.

In several places the timber had cracked and been repaired by patches of wood. Two such, one nearly thirty-two inches long, the other five inches and a half long, have been figured on Plate IV. Fig. 31 and 32. On their inner surface, there are vestiges of the caulking material, consisting of woollen woven stuff, and a pitchy kind of substance similar to that used for fixing the feathers on the arrows.

In and near this boat were found a pair of poles like those found in the oak boat, and a number of the pieces figured on Plate III. Fig. 23, and on Plate IV. Fig. 26, such as were also found in the oak boat; as well as a wooden water-conduit (of which it was impossible to determine the length, as only a part could be exhumed); on one side of which the outline of an animal was roughly carved (Plate IV. Fig. 28); and finally, two wooden scoops (Plate IV. Fig. 35 and 36), one of which was in fragments sufficient only to show its size, the handle alone being entire. The boat contained several vessels of wood, amongst which a large tray, seventeen inches and a half long by four inches deep inside, the thickness of the wood being half an inch (Plate XIV. Fig. 25); further, many fragments of damascened swords, many metal fittings for sheaths, the sheath for a knife (Plate XV. Fig. 1); a wooden quiver (Plate XIII. Fig. 63); a wooden club (Plate XV. Fig. 15); a basket of bast, containing a net (Plate XIV. Fig. 14); a crow-bar, and several other objects. In the fore-end some shafts of lances were found, and outside the boat, close under one of its sides, lay a thick board eight to ten feet long and one foot and a half broad, but it is not clear for what it was used. The objects of iron found in the boat had suffered much from rust.

The boats here described I consider to have been merely rowing-boats, not destined to carry sails, and in forming this opinion, I rely principally on the fact that neither masts nor any signs of rigging have been discovered, nor any arrangements in the boats for fixing the necessary ropes. It is true that in the middle of the bottom plank of the oak boat, as well as of the fir boat, there is a hole of about one inch and a half diameter, but these holes are too small to have carried masts, and may have served for letting out water when the boats were hauled on shore, as was probably the case at the beginning of the winter.

The discovery of these boats at Nydam affords the first recorded instance of the remains of ancient ships being so well preserved as to render the reconstruction of a complete ship possible. It is true that such remains are known to have been found in tumuli, both in Scandinavia (at Ultuna,* and at Lackalänga,† in Sweden, at Borre,‡ near Horten, in Norway), and in England, viz. at Snape, in Suffolk,§ where a boat was dug out forty feet eight inches long, nine feet six inches wide, and three feet ten inches deep, clincher-built (seven nails occupying a space of three feet, that is, about the same as in the Nydam boats), and containing some human hair, a gold ring with a Roman engraved gem, and fragments of a glass vessel with projections at the sides, of a shape similar to that found in the boat discovered at Borre, and known from several graves in England, France, and Germany, belonging to the later part of the Iron age. (See C. Roach Smith's Coll. Ant. vol. ii. pl. li.; Cochet, Normandie Souterraine, pl. x., etc.)

From the accounts of these discoveries of ships in tumuli, it appears that they were clincher built, but the form and other details were not observed, nor indeed could it be expected that much should remain of boats buried in tumuli. So much, however,

---

* B. E. Hildebrand's account in the report of the seventh meeting of Scandinavian Naturalists, Kris-tiania, 1856, Appendix, p. 644.

† Described by N. G. Bruzelius in the 'Annaler for Nordisk Oldkyndighed,' 1858, p. 179.

‡ Described by Nicolaysen in the Report for 1852 of the Society for the Preservation of Norwegian Antiquities.

§ Davidson, in the Proceedings of the Society of Antiquaries, 2nd series, vols. ii.–iv. p. 177.

may be considered certain, that all these instances of ships buried in tumuli belong to the last division of the Iron period.

Nor is it possible to derive any certain knowledge from the so-called "skibssætninger," rows of stones set so as to form the outline of a boat, as in the annexed chemitype, and which probably were the burial-places of Vikings; nor from the representations of boats on Runic sculptured stones, which, like the "skibssætninger" and the tumuli just mentioned, belong to the latter part of the Iron age. They are too rude to give an insight into details of structure; and the same is the case with the so-called "hällristningar," engraved on the sides of rocks and on large stones in Scandinavia, and I suppose also in England. These last figures present the additional difficulty, that their age is not to be determined with any degree of certainty.

Similar and equally rude representations of boats have been found even on bronze implements, presumably older than the boats of Nydam, —for instance, on the knife found in Ditmarsh, and copied below from Kemble's 'Horæ Ferales,' p. 228.

Hollowed trunks have been used at all times, and are still used on many rivers and lakes, and, no doubt, afforded the earliest means of crossing such waters, but even if it were possible to determine the age of those which have been found embedded in sand and mud at the bottom of rivers and inland lakes, we could not, of course, gather from them any information as to the ancient principles of naval architecture properly speaking.

From all this it follows that neither with regard to the Bronze age, nor with regard to the later part of the Iron age, do we possess any information on this subject which in any way could render a comparison possible between the ship-building of those periods and the state of this art during the Early Iron age in Denmark, so fully and surprisingly illustrated by the boats discovered at Nydam.

## 2. WEARING APPAREL.

(Thorsbjerg, Plates 1–3.)

The number of objects belonging to this class is not considerable, but they give, nevertheless, a good idea of the dress of those times, though only as regards the men ; for neither in this bog nor in any of the others, where similar deposits occur, has anything been found distinctly connected with female dress or female occupations.

1. Two *Cloaks* were found at Thorsbjerg, each made of a square piece of woollen cloth, woven in a twill-pattern, the lower edge adorned with a border and fringe. The pattern is shown in Plate 2, Fig. 4. They measure fifty-two by forty-one inches. One is of a dark-brown colour, owing to the tanning influence of the bog-water; the original colour cannot now be determined. The other shows a greenish colour at the bottom, the fringe being yellow and black. Several fragments of woven cloth with borders and fringes, belonged seemingly to similar cloaks; among them is a specimen of remarkably fine texture, a piece of which is shown in Plate 2, Fig. 5.

2. A *Kirtle* of woollen woven cloth, thirty-four inches and a half long and twenty-one inches broad (Plate 1), composed of two pieces, the seams being sewn with black woollen thread of three plies. Fig. *b* represents the border below. The sleeves have separately woven borders of a very fine and elegant texture, a piece of which is represented in Fig. *c*. The sleeves, moreover, are made of another, and, I presume on account of their being exposed to wear, stronger sort of cloth, with a diamond pattern— Fig. *a*—resembling that of the stockings in Plate 2. This jacket is a very good instance of the singular state of preservation of many of these objects, though one of the sleeves was almost torn away, and the kirtle itself had many and large rents.

3. Two pairs of long *Trowsers* of woollen cloth, somewhat coarser than the above-mentioned garments. The stockings of another and finer cloth than these, and woven with a diamond pattern, are sewn to them. The best-preserved specimen is forty-six inches and a half long and forty inches round the waist; the length of the foot eleven inches and a half. These measures indicate a strongly-built man of more than average height. At the waist are several straps through which the belt was fastened. This pair of trowsers was found rolled up; their condition when unrolled is shown by Fig. 1 in Plate 2.

4. *Leather Coverings for the Feet.*—A leather sandal in a single piece for the left foot, discovered at Thorsbjerg, is represented on Plate 3, Fig. 1. It is stitched together at the heel, and tightened around the toe by means of straps, and, perhaps, buttons; its length from heel to toe is nearly eleven inches; under the sole two long impressions in the leather are observable, indicating the place in which an additional sole had been fastened. On one side of the heel is still preserved a little silver-plated

bronze rivet, probably intended for the strap of the spur. The ornaments appear to be of a quasi-Roman style. Another simpler and coarser sandal, without ornaments, was found, and some fragments of others, one of which was furnished along the edge of the sole with a row of nails with silver-plated heads.

It is extremely rare to find any wearing apparel among the relics of ancient times, and this is the only known specimen of a tolerably complete dress of the third century A.C. From the Bronze age we fortunately possess a perfect suit of woollen cloth, found upon a skeleton in an oaken trunk in a barrow called Treenhöi, parish of Vamdrup, and preserved in the Copenhagen Museum.* Compared with this earlier dress, the garments now discovered indicate a much higher skill in weaving. Sandals of Roman origin, much like those here found, have been frequently discovered in the Thames,† and the bogs of Ireland have yielded many specimens that correspond with ours in shape.‡

### 3. PERSONAL ORNAMENTS AND ARTICLES OF THE TOILET.

### (Thorsbjerg, Plate 4, and Nydam, Plate V.)

1. *Fibulæ* are of frequent occurrence in Denmark during both the Bronze and the Iron periods. They present great variety in shape and ornamentation, and are found not only of simple forms and common materials, but—especially those of later date—of costly metals, and adorned in a very magnificent manner. More than sixty specimens were brought to light in Thorsbjerg, in two varieties of shape, circular and bowed. The former are rare in Denmark, and only two were found in Thorsbjerg; they are made of bronze, plated with gold and silver, and furnished with concentric rings of very elegant small silver beads, an ornamentation highly characteristic of this period (Plate 4, Fig. 6 and 7). The other fibulæ from Thorsbjerg were of the bowed form, the principal varieties of which are shown in Plate 4, Fig. 1–5 and 8–13. Many of them are ornamented with thin plates of precious metals. From Nydam we have only nine fibulæ, all of heavier and less elegant forms than the Thorsbjerg specimens (Plate V. Fig. 12–14). The common forms are well known among the contents of Danish tumuli of this period.

2. Two silver *Clasps*, from Nydam, one set with blue glass, are figured on Plate V. Fig. 1–2.

* Good drawings of the contents of this barrow are given in Mr. Madsen's ' Afbildninger,' an ably-illustrated work on our antiquities, to which I wish to draw the attention of archæologists.

† See C. R. Smith's ' Catalogue of the Museum of London Antiquities,' 1854, p. 67.

‡ Compare Sir W. R. Wilde's ' Catalogue of the Antiquities in the Museum of the Royal Irish Academy,' p. 281 et seqq.

3. The originals of Plate 4, Fig. 17–20, and of Plate V. Fig. 19–21, have probably been *Buttons ;* they are too large, it seems, to have served as beads, and have besides, a flat and unornamented base, while beads are usually ornamented all over. The buttons, Plate V. Fig. 19 and 20, are particularly remarkable for their resemblance to the well-known urns from old English cemeteries. (Compare Nydam, Plate XIV. Fig. 22.)

4. The chief types of the *Beads* are shown in Plate 4, Fig. 22–24, and Nydam, Plate V. Fig. 18 and 22. They are either of agate or made of opaque or transparent glass, or vitrified porcelain. These are sometimes of the same material throughout, sometimes made of stems of glass of many different colours, so combined as to form a variegated whole. Sometimes the designs are produced by melting enamel of various colours into grooves made on the surface of the beads. Beads of this description are widely diffused all over Europe and the East, but, at least in Denmark, they were not in common use prior to the first appearance of iron. Through the Iron period they appear to have been a common article of commerce, being very similar in all countries. Those here mentioned, for instance, will be easily recognised as resembling specimens found in England.

5. Two bronze spiral *Finger-rings*, of three coils (Plate 4, Fig. 16).

6. Among the fragments of gold rings, cut to pieces in order to serve as ring-money, six were discovered to have formed originally a *Bracelet* (see the subjoined figure). The other fragments of rings will be mentioned under the head of ring-money (Plate 16).

7. Attention must be drawn to some small bronze and silver *Pendants* in the form of weights (Plate 18, Fig. 3, and Nydam, Plate V. Fig. 15 and 16), and in one instance shaped like a little basket (Nydam, Plate V. Fig. 17). Similar pendants have been lately discovered in Vimose, to the number of six, hanging on a bronze ring, five inches in diameter. They may perhaps have been filled with a heavy substance, and have served as weights; in Vimose we discovered scales of bronze very like the ordinary form of the present day.

8. A little *Bulla* of gold is figured on Plate 4, No. 14, which shows the reverse, with nine holes, forming an irregular cross. The front is hollow and was perhaps originally filled with a precious stone, or a piece of coloured glass, now lost.

9. A gold *Drop-ornament* (Plate 4, Fig. 15) was the only one found here, though they are of frequent occurrence in Denmark and in the northern part of Germany.*

10. *Combs* of bone were found in Nydam, but not in Thorsbjerg. They are made of one piece, as Plate V. Fig. 10, or composed of two pieces, as is the case in Fig. 11 in Plate V. where the small rivets are of iron, or of many pieces, as Fig. 9 in the same

* Many specimens are figured in the Meklenburgische Jahrbücher.

Plate. One comb was found in a bronze buckler, another in a vessel of clay, discovered in the oak boat.

11. *Tweezers* of bronze and silver were often found on the same ring with ear-picks (Plate 4, Fig. 25 and 26, and Nydam, Plate V. Fig. 3, 4, 6–8).

12. Among the objects of the toilet may also be classed a double-barrelled *Silver Box* (Nydam, Plate V. Fig. 5), which may have been an ointment pot, and appears to have been hung on the same ring with Fig. 4 and 6. Certain small *Boxes* (Thorsbjerg, Plate 17, Fig. 6, and Nydam, Plate XIV. Fig. 15–17) may belong to the same class.

---

### 4. A DIE OF AMBER.

(Thorsbjerg, Plate 4, Fig. 27.)

The edges of this die are rounded, so that it cannot stand on 1 and 6; the numbers are marked by means of concentric circles. This is the only object of the kind which has been found in Slesvig, though draughtsmen are frequent elsewhere, and a draught-board was found at Vimose.

---

### 5. ARMS OF DEFENCE.

These have been found in considerable numbers, and are among the most important objects discovered in the mosses. Helmets, coats of mail, swords and shields of Gothic origin, were formerly unknown of so early a date; they are now illustrated by good specimens discovered in these deposits. Other defensive armour, as greaves and vambraces, have not been found; nor does it appear from the accounts of historians that such were commonly, or even occasionally, used among the Goths. We shall endeavour to point out, under each head, what must be assigned to Roman, or at least Romanized workmanship and art, and what, judging from shape and style of ornament, belongs to the Goths. The former will be found to be very few, compared with the latter.

#### a. *Coverings for the Head.*

(Thorsbjerg, Plate 5.)

It is probable from the accounts of historians, that the head-coverings of the so-called barbarian nations were of light and perishable materials, and this may explain their very rare occurrence in those graves in which weapons have been deposited with the dead.  Procopius (de Bello Gothico, i. 21) indicates the high rank of a man among the Goths by telling us that he wore a helmet.  Among the Heruli, only the king, it would seem, was permitted to wear this piece of armour. (Warnefried, de Gestis Longobard. i. 20.)  In the poem of Beówulf, helmets are often mentioned; the circumstance, however, that they have individual names seems to show that they were held in high estimation, and probably worn only by persons of high rank, not by common soldiers.  Even among the Romans, helmets were not in universal use.  Vegetius, in the latter part of the fourth century, says that, according to old custom, the light infantry wore caps made of hides.

With this information, gathered from written sources, the discoveries of antiquities entirely agree.  A richly ornamented helmet of bronze was discovered in 1862, in an ancient channel of the Seine, and is now preserved in the Louvre.  It was described in ' Revue Archéologique' for 1862, and spoken of as having probably belonged to some of the Oriental chiefs following Attila on his expedition against the Western Empire.  Mr. Franks has lately,* with great propriety, assigned it a place among a great many corresponding objects belonging to the Late Celtic period.

Another headpiece, formed of iron ribs, was found in a barrow of inconsiderable elevation—about six feet from a skeleton—on the farm called Benty Grange, near Monyash, in Derbyshire; it belongs to a late period, probably the sixth or seventh century.†

In Scandinavia several instances are known of iron helmets having been found in tumuli in which boats were deposited, and which appear, from their contents, to have been the burial-places of men of very high rank.  These also are of a much later time —the last period of heathendom.

The Nydam deposit has only yielded some very questionable fragments of helmets (Plate V. Fig. 23 to 27); and all the objects hereafter described as belonging to helmets have been found in Thorsbjerg.

1. Fig. 1 in Plate 5 represents a fragment of the back of a *Roman Helmet* of thin bronze.  A great many smaller fragments found along with it indubitably belong to the same helmet, but we have not succeeded in restoring it further than is shown in the drawing.  The workmanship, no less than the ornaments imitating flames, the thunderbolt, and the star, surrounded by a wreath, suffice at a glance to mark its purely Roman origin.

2. The *Bronze Serpent*, of which the engraving, Fig. 2, gives a good idea, once probably ornamented a Roman helmet.  Remains of a soldering material are left on the under surface.

* See Kemble, ' Horæ Ferales,' London, 1863, p. 174.
† Bateman, ' Ten Years' Diggings,' London, 1861, p. 28; and C. R. Smith, ' Collectanea Antiqua,' ii. p. 238.

3. Fig. 3 in Plate 5 represents an extremely remarkable *Silver Helmet*, unique among all the objects of the Early Iron age. It is composed of two pieces, the mask for the face and the crown, which latter is shown separately in Fig. 4. They are fastened together by a moveable hinge with three rivets. The mask is of silver, lined with bronze plates, and externally, in many places, covered with thin gold plates. It weighs, in its present imperfect state, about a pound and a half. The neck-piece is formed of thin silver ribs plated with gold, and decorated in the same manner as the visor. The imitations of birds' heads as ornaments occur very frequently on objects from the peat-mosses, and exclusively, I believe, on objects dating from this period, of which they may therefore be considered characteristic, nor are they as yet known from other countries. (Compare especially Thorsbjerg, Plate 10, Fig. 36 and 37, and Fig. *a*, in page 19, of a belt-loop of a scabbard from Vimose; see also Thorsbjerg, Plate 15, Fig. 27, and Plate 18, Fig. 8.)

4. The use of the *Curved Plate*, figured in No. 47, Plate 11, one of the gems of the Flensborg collection, has not been ascertained. It has most probably decorated the front of a helmet, like the last mentioned. But whatever its use, it is an interest-
ing object, on account of the embossed figures represented on it, affording good evidence of the advanced art of the Goths at the time of their arrival in Denmark. The art, indeed, is " barbarous," but yet by no means undeveloped. The annexed woodcut shows the profile, half-size. The piece is composed of a thick bronze plate, with the rims bent up, and externally plated with silver and gold, in which representations of animals are worked in relief by the aid of dies. Above and below are two rows of human heads in profile, covered with a curious sort of helmet with ear-flaps; every alternate head is plated with gold, and all are struck from the same die. The five principal animals in the centre are a hippocampus, a capricorn, a wild boar (the Gullinbörste perhaps, of Northern mytho- logy), a bird, probably the raven of Odin, and the last, from its posture, a fox or a wolf. The interstices between these larger animals are filled with smaller figures of fishes, and a lizard with cleft tail and open mouth. A glance at the engraving will prove, that the style of art does not show the least trace of Roman influence; it is rather, we should say, Oriental, and has many features in common with that of the celebrated golden horns found at Gallehuus, in the parish of Mögeltönder, South Jutland, unfortunately stolen some sixty years ago.

### b. *Chain Armour.*

(Thorsbjerg, Plates 6 and 7.)

The chain armour found at Thorsbjerg (at Nydam no relics of this kind have been discovered) is composed of interlinked iron rings, generally in alternate rows of riveted and welded rings, so that four riveted rings are fitted into one welded ring, and *vice versâ;* occasionally, however, all the rings are riveted, and in one instance the rivets are of bronze, whilst the rings are of iron. The rings average a little less than half an inch in diameter. Borders for the sleeves and the lower part of the hauberk, of very elegant riveted rings of bronze, were also found, showing the ordinary circumference of the hauberk to be forty inches, and that of the sleeves, eighteen inches and a half. Five or six specimens of hauberks of this description were met with, all of them rolled up; sometimes they contained small fragments of iron swords and mountings in bronze, appertaining to various other weapons, and in two instances they were placed in vessels of burnt clay—circumstances which clearly show that these things were intentionally deposited in the moss. The coats of mail being much corroded, we are left in ignorance of their shape; but we may presume from representations on Roman monuments of about the same period, that they reached to above the knees, and that the sleeves were short.

These, as well as the breast-plates and buckles belonging to them, are of Roman workmanship, yet, as will be shown hereafter, they also testify to an intercourse between the Romans and the Goths.

It is evident that the *Breastplates* represented by Fig. 1 in Plate 6, and Fig. 7 in Plate 7 are of Roman, or perhaps rather Romanized manufacture; the art is of no very high character, and we are inclined to consider them as having been copied from better models by barbarian artificers in the service of Roman armourers. The dies for the Medusa-heads, in open work, surrounding the inner boss, those for the helmeted warrior sitting or half-reclining in his chair, with his sword before him, and leaning his left hand on a buckler, as well as the dies for the small genii, and the various animals on the outer rim, as, birds, serpents, dolphins, and hippocampi (which are repeated many times), are all certainly fashioned after Roman prototypes. On the other hand, however, it is evident that the eight small figures—fishes, birds, horses, and mythical animals,—each fastened by two rivets to the angles of each of the four compartments of the plate, did not originally belong to it; nor have they been applied as restorations, for in the upper compartment, from which they were removed after the plate was found, in order that the original might be seen in its entirety, no defect or mark is to be observed, except the four holes for the reception of the rivets of Fig. 1 *c* and 1 *d*. These small animal figures are undeniably *barbarian*, even in comparison with the breastplate, and we cannot account for this, otherwise than by presuming that the plate must have fallen into the hands of a people, to whom the small figures, which had been afterwards riveted to the plate, bore a symbolical meaning, or were at least pleasing and tasteful as decorations.

The breastplate, represented by Fig. 7, may perhaps originally have corresponded to that last described. The platings of the outer rim may at some time have been torn off, and in its stead a plate with embossed figures of animals have been applied. Enough of this outer rim is left to give an idea of the whole. The same representation of three different animals, with a dolphin between them,—the first and the last of the four larger animals preserved being from the same die,—has doubtless been repeated round the whole outer rim, as we often find to be the case in representations of this kind; for instance, on a silver goblet from Himlingöie, in Sealand, represented in Worsaae's Antiquities, p. 77. The arrangement of the figures on the gold-plated upper rim is shown on the annexed woodcuts, full size.

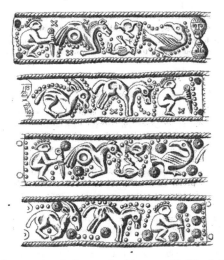

The breastplates consist of a framework of bronze, with thin platings of gold and silver. Their diameter is five inches.

Besides the breastplates, four pairs of buckles, examples of which are figured in Nos. 4–6, and 8, in Plates 6 and 7, evidently belong to hauberks.

Coats of mail, it is believed, were introduced into Europe from Eastern countries;

they were in common use in the fourteenth century, but the elegant manufacture of riveted rings has been hitherto regarded as unknown prior to the fifteenth century. The coat of mail of the early middle age, as it is seen for instance on the Bayeux tapestry, is usually regarded as having consisted of iron rings fastened on to a leather jacket; but as chain-armour has now been found associated with antiquities of the third century, we are justified in believing it to have been known in the earliest period of the middle ages.

It is, nevertheless, probable that such armour must have been very precious and rare, even among classic nations. According to a Greek author of the middle of the second century B.C., only those wore such ring-mail who possessed more than ten thousand drachms, the less opulent covering their breasts with plates of metal (Polybius, vi. 21). From representations on Roman sepulchral slabs, of the first centuries of the Christian era, we see that coats of mail were used, but we cannot determine whether the rings were riveted or not.

In Northern countries, no previous discoveries of ancient chain-mail of an earlier date have been made. A fragment of interlinked rings was found with a human skeleton outside the gate of St. Severinus at Cologne.[*] It appears, however, from the other relics discovered with it, to be of a somewhat later date than ours.

### c. *Shields.*

### (Thorsbjerg, Plate 8.)

Shields formed an important part of the military equipment; they were circular and flat, their diameter ranging from twenty-two inches and a half to forty-four inches. In the centre was the opening for the hand, the usual shape of which is seen in Fig. 4; the wooden handle (Fig. 5) was inserted across the opening, and fitted into a notch on each side of it. Various metal coverings for the wooden handles are represented in Fig. 6–10. In front of the opening was the boss of metal, concave on the inside. Rims of metal usually protected the edges (Fig. 19–22 and Fig. 32). The mountings, several varieties of which are represented in Fig. 23–31, served for repairs, and perhaps also for decorations.

A great many *Boards*, once portion of shields, were found in both mosses, separately as well as in layers one on the other, and, as already stated, sometimes transfixed by javelins, as if to keep the whole together. Boards thus fixed together did not however, by any means usually belong to the same shield, and in spite of the great number of single boards preserved, we have only succeeded in making up three complete wooden shields, one of which is represented by Fig. 1. These suffice, however, in connexion with the many fragments, to show the details of the framework.

---

[*] See 'Collectanea Antiqua,' vol. ii. 148.

The boards, varying in breadth from three to nine inches and a half, are smoothly planed, and traces of the planing tool are clearly seen in many places: their average thickness is represented in Fig. 2 and 3. They are of a soft sort of wood, probably alder; occasionally also oak or deal boards were found, though these latter were very rare.

How the eight or ten boards, of which the shield was composed, were kept together, we cannot tell. One fragment with a covering of thin leather, and only one, was brought to light, but such a cover appears insufficient to hold the boards in their places, even if we presume that the shields were usually strengthened in this manner. In one instance only, among the many hundred boards which were found, small square pieces of wood (or dowels) projected from the edges so as to fit into notches made in the next board. On one board, traces of an iron mounting were found, but its form could not be recognised, the iron being much corroded. With these few and doubtful exceptions, no trace is left of the manner in which the boards were kept together; the weak cylindrical metal rim does not seem sufficient for this purpose.

The *Handles* of wood were fastened to the shield by wooden pegs, the metallic coverings by rivets of iron or bronze. (See Fig. 5–10 in Plate 8, and the annexed chemitype.)

Wooden handle from Nydam. ½.

The *Bosses* were made of iron and bronze, rarely of silver, wood, or wicker-work. As the iron in Thorsbjerg moss has been decomposed by the peat-water, no bosses of this metal have been preserved there, though some small fragments indicate that they once existed, and from their frequent occurrence at Nydam, where the water is less corrosive, we may even conclude that iron bosses have been abundant at Thorsbjerg also.

The annexed chemitype shows the usual form of the iron bosses found at Nydam, which were more than sixty in number, and for the most part provided with thin bronze rims. A very few umbones of bronze, hammered very thin from a single piece of metal, and of the same shape as those of iron, were also found at that place. The costliest of the bosses

½.

from Nydam consisted of an iron frame covered with a thin plate of silver, overlaid with a thin plate of gold without ornaments.

The majority of the bosses from Thorsbjerg are of bronze, and of two kinds.

1. Fig. 11 and 12 represent good examples of the six bosses of Roman origin found here; their diameter varies from six to seven inches; the metal is commonly thicker than that of the other kind. On one is an inscription in dotted Roman letters, AEL. AELIANVS.* It may be the name of the owner, or that of the general, for

---

* The names occur on a sepulchral slab in the Lateran church at Rome. See Muratori 'Novus Thesaurus Veterum Inscriptionum,' p. 1126, n. 2. See also Gruter, 697, 7. Similar repetitions occur in the names Æmilius Æmilianus, Fabius Fabianus, Vibius Vibianus, etc.

H

it was common in the later times of the republic, and during the first centuries A.C., for the Roman soldiers to inscribe the name of the general on their shield-bosses. (See Mr. A. W. Franks, " On Bosses of Roman Shields," Archæological Journal, 1858, vol. xv. p. 55.)

2. Those of the other kind, of which sixteen have been found, are of Gothic origin. They average six inches and a quarter in diameter. The metal is surprisingly thin, so as to render it probable that many of them have been furnished with some inner support. The edges have almost always been protected by metal rims. The chief peculiarity of these bosses consists in an opening at their top for the reception of a hollow or massive spike—as shown by Figs. 17 and 18 in Plate 18, the use of which I had not found out at the time when the plate was engraved. Some have also a mounting of the kind represented in Fig. 14, Plate 8, fastened by a rivet on the inner side of the hollow. Another variety is shown in the annexed woodcut of a fragment of a silver boss from Thorsbjerg.

Two objects which have obviously served as inner supports for such thin bosses of metal have been preserved. One in size and shape perfectly resembles the bosses of metal, but is made of comparatively thick wood.* The other, the original of Fig. 15 (Plate 8), is composed of wicker-work. That these bosses are of Gothic origin, is probable from the workmanship, the peculiarities of form, and a Runic inscription on one of them ; as well as from the ornamental details and the style of art of the fragment figured in Fig. 18 (Plate 8.). The latter presents some peculiarities worthy

‡.

of notice. Representations of living forms for decorative purposes were at this period usually either worked in relief by the aid of a die, or engraved in the metal as is the case on a bronze vessel found at Baunshöi (Worsaae's Ant. fig. 302). On the fragment in question, however, the indented ornaments and the figures of animals are cut out of a very thin gold plate, and then soldered to the silver boss. The Runic inscription occurs on the inner side of the outer rim of one of the very thin bronze bosses, it consists of six distinct letters engraved rather carelessly with a pointed tool (Plate 8, Fig. 16).†

Commonly, the shields have been provided with rims consisting of thin plates of bronze, or more rarely, of silver, fastened round the edge by rivets through the metal itself, or through small projecting roundels. (Plate 8, Fig. 19–22, and the annexed figure a.) A few shields have been found without any appearance of having been strengthened in this manner. Traces of old repairs and restorations have, as we might expect, been often found not only on the thin metal bosses, but also on the wooden shields. The

* In the course of the diggings in Vimose, in Fyen, in 1865, no less than five wooden umbones were found.
† The runes have been read by the Rev. D. Haigh as AISC AH (Aisc owns). See 'Archæological Journal,' 1863, vol. xx. p. 298.

various forms of metal mountings used for the latter purpose may be seen in Plate 8, Fig. 23–31, especially in Figs. 23 and 23 *a*, the wood having been in this instance preserved. Compare also the two annexed figures *b* and *c*.

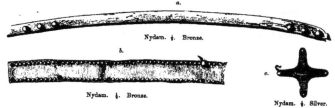

a.

Nydam. ⅓. Bronze.

b.

Nydam. ⅓. Bronze.

c.

Nydam. ⅓. Silver.

Having met with Roman bosses among the antiquities from these excavations, we might naturally expect also to light upon Roman shields. But all the fragments, without a single exception, indicate shields of the above description, and none agree either with the square and convex shield (*scutum*), or with the oval and hollow shield (*clypeus*) of the Romans, such as are described by historians of the second century, and are represented on the triumphal arches of the later emperors.

There is another and very important difference, viz. as to the manner in which the shields were carried. The Roman shield, it is well known, had two loops on the inner side, one for the arm to pass through, the other for the hand. The Gothic shield, on the contrary, was intended to be held in the left hand before the body; the warrior's skill and dexterity was shown by handling it so as to catch the javelins and darts of the enemy, and in close combat so as to protect the body against the blows of swords and axes. In this respect, the following account of one of the last battles between the Romans and the Goths in Italy, in the vicinity of Mount Vesuvius, is of interest. The king, says Procopius, De Bello Gothico, A.D. 553, " stood covered by his shield in the front of the little band of warriors that was left. The Romans attacked him, hoping that his death would decide the battle in their favour. The king of the Goths caught the missiles with his shield, and occasionally he rushed forward and killed one of his opponents. When he observed that the weight of the javelins bore down his shield, he called to his attendant to give him another. After he had thus fought about the third part of the day, it happened that twelve javelins were sticking in his shield, so that it was difficult for him to move it, and at the same time keep the enemy at a distance. He accordingly called to his attendant, without stirring from the spot. With his sword in his right hand he carried havoc among the enemy, while he kept back those that thronged upon him by the aid of the shield in his left hand. But while changing his shield, his breast for a moment was left uncovered, and a javelin pierced him."

H 2

In the poem of Beówulf, the shield is called " the refuge of warriors," " the wondrous war-board," and other names that obviously show the great importance attaching to it at that time. And yet the thin wooden shield with which we become acquainted from the peat-mosses, must have been a very weak defence. Nor were the shields of a later period of Northern antiquity stronger than these. In Kormak's Saga, for instance, we read that each of the warriors in a single combat had three shields at his disposal, carried by an attendant, and when these were shattered, they had to finish the combat with their swords.

---

### 6. OFFENSIVE WEAPONS.

The principal kinds of offensive weapons known to antiquity, such as swords, spears, bows and arrows, are represented in our moss-deposits, and many specimens are in a fine state of preservation. We shall first consider—

#### a. *Swords.*

(Thorsbjerg, Plates 9–11, and Nydam, Plates VI.–IX.)

The peat-water, as I have before observed, had decomposed almost all the iron objects of the Thorsbjerg deposit; only a few fragments of iron blades remained, and these much oxidized; a dark streak, hardly discernible in the peat, was, in most instances, all that was left. Occasionally small fragments, wrapped up in chain-mail, were discovered, but from these it was impossible to infer anything as to the form and manufacture of the weapon.

Fortunately, the discovery of more than a hundred swords in Nydam moss supplied this deficiency.

The Nydam swords are of iron, long, straight, and two-edged; the blades are for the most part—ninety out of a hundred—richly damascened in various patterns, and afford good illustrations of the poet's sword, " the costliest of irons, with twisted hilt, and variegated like a snake" (Beówulf). Iron wires, arranged in patterns, have been laid in grooves made in the surface of the blades, and then the whole has been welded together, so that the surface must originally have been smooth. That we now see the patterns raised is probably owing to unequal oxidation. Among the many elegant and ingenious patterns represented on Plates VI. and VII., I would call special attention to Fig. 5 and 5a, with borders of flowers freely rendered in twisted iron wire.

It is no uncommon thing to find the blades ground hollow (compare Fig. 3 a, 12 a, and 19 a), but blades with facets (Fig. 14), and without damascening are, as I have already observed, very rare in this deposit. Neither has a single curved sword or seax, such as are frequent at Vimose (see p. 20), been discovered in the two Slesvig mosses.

The Nydam swords are between thirty and forty inches long; the blades are one inch and a half to two inches and three-quarters broad near the hilt, from which the breadth gradually decreases until about one inch from the point.

On the tangs and blades of some of the Nydam swords are found different stamps (Fig. 2, 14, 18, and 22), and inscriptions with raised Roman letters in sunk squares, RICVS (Fig. 18), RICCIM (Fig. 20), COCILLVS (Fig. 21), VMORCD (Fig. 22).* Inscriptions, which, on account of the oxidized state of the iron, cannot be read, occur on three other tangs.

On the original of Fig. 18 we have the number xx., and on the blade of a broad sword without damascening (Fig. 17), two figures resembling Runic letters are inlaid with golden wire (Fig. 17a); they stand on a conspicuous part of the blade, and probably may have had a magic signification.

In Thorsbjerg was discovered a wooden sword (see Plate 9, Fig. 3), which has attracted the special attention of antiquaries, for it is, oddly enough, not the only wooden weapon found in the mosses. In the same depository there was a spear-head of wood, and the excavations of Vimose in 1865 also brought to light a wooden sword. These weapons cannot have had a warlike destination, but may have been used for the practice of recruits, as Polybius mentions (x. 2) that wooden swords, over which a leather covering was stretched, were used for such purposes.† Nevertheless we should perhaps rather consider those found in our mosses as votive offerings to the gods, intended to take the place of the real weapons.

*Hilts of swords* were dug up in surprisingly great numbers; with only one exception, those from Thorsbjerg are made of wood; nearly all have metal ornaments, or are mounted with plates or nails of metal. The greater portion are of the description figured in Figs. 1 and 2 on Plate 9. Most probably they have all been covered with leather, stretched over them while it was yet wet. They consist of three pieces:—the pommel, for varieties of which see Fig. 9, 11, 13, and 14, the grip, and the hemispherical piece below (see Fig. 8, 12, 15, and 19). They are, it will be seen, differently ornamented. The exception alluded to above is a fragment of a very magnificent hilt, of which two pieces remain (Fig. 10 and 10 b), consisting of bronze plated with gold and silver. This form of the hilt is commonly seen on sepulchral monuments dating from the decline of the empire.

Another variety of hilt, represented by various figures on Plate VI., and Fig. 5 in Plate 9, was of much rarer occurrence in Thorsbjerg, but very common in Nydam. These consist of cylindrical pieces of wood, with plates of bronze and silver, and sometimes also of bone, the two cross-pieces above and below being quite similar in shape.

---

* The fourth letter may be ɤ instead of R, and the sixth ɤ instead of D.

† Compare also Vegetius, ' De Re Militari,' vol. i. 11.

Many specimens of this description are known from Kragehul (p. 21) (Worsaae's Ant. no. 330). Another found in a barrow near Sætrang, in Norway, is described in the 'Annaler for Nordisk Oldkyndighed,' 1836–37, and a very similar specimen found in a barrow at Coombe, in Kent, is described in C. Roach Smith's 'Collectanea Antiqua,' vol. ii. 164.

The wooden hilt, figured in Plate 9, No. 4, is hitherto unique. The aperture below, shown in Fig. 4 a, would appear to indicate a single-edged sword-blade with a broad back, though no such swords have been discovered in the turbary deposits of South Jutland, but only in the Vimose in Fyen.

The *Sheaths* were composed of two very thin wooden laths, held together at the edges by mountings either of wood, partly cut out of the same piece with the front lath, or of metal. Among the latter, two varieties may be distinguished. Of one variety only two specimens were discovered, represented on Plate 10, Fig. 31 and 42. The swords to which they belonged were evidently of early Roman, or at least Romanized form, short and broad, and the mountings of the sheaths are also of Romanized work and style, different from the others dug up in the same locality. The original of Fig. 31 was cut in two, one half was laid on the other, an additional proof, if any were needed, that the objects were deposited intentionally. Of the hundred swords that were brought to light by the diggings in Nydam moss, not a single one would fit such scabbards as these which were found at Thorsbjerg.

The ordinary sheath, of which Plate VIII., Fig. 26, will convey an idea, is narrower and longer than the last mentioned. From some fragments it would appear that they were sometimes covered with leather. The laths of which they are composed are mostly so thin, and were so saturated with water, that it was only with great difficulty some fragments could be taken up from the great depth at which they were laid, and preserved. Many of the mountings are distinguished for their tasteful forms and elegant workmanship. I beg to draw attention to the chapes, and the mountings for the middle of the sheath, forming a loop through which the thin end of the sword-belt (see Plate 11, Fig. 48) was passed for the purpose of suspending the sheath. Many examples of them are shown in Plates 9–10 and VIII.-IX. The more costly ones are manufactured in a manner characteristic of this period, a plate of bronze being decorated with a thin casing of precious metal, in which various ornaments are wrought. The original of Plate IX., Fig. 44 of iron, with a pattern inlaid with gold wire, is hitherto unique among our antiquities. The patterns, it would seem, are quite Pompeiian.

The original of the chape (Fig. 41, Thorsbjerg, Plate 10) has a Runic inscription of two lines, one on each side, and each consisting of ten letters.* This inscription is written in the earlier Runic alphabet, which was in use prior to that found on most of the Runic stones in Denmark, almost all of which date from the last centuries of heathenism. This earlier alphabet differs from the later in the shapes of several runes, and but few of the

---

* See the 'Archæological Journal,' 1863, vol. xx. p. 298.

inscriptions have hitherto been satisfactorily read. They have in Denmark been found chiefly on portable objects, and eleven instances of such are known, besides many on bracteates.[*] It would, however, in my opinion be a mistake, if from the circumstance that large monuments with the earlier Runic letters have not hitherto been discovered in our country, we should infer that the portable objects we have mentioned have belonged to a people which only passed through the land on their way to another country. It appears from the contents of the graves, and their frequent occurrence in all parts of Denmark, that the people to whom these relics must be assigned settled regularly, and remained here for a long period.

Girdles and shoulder-belts of leather were of very rare occurrence. Fig. 48 in Plate 11 represents a shoulder-belt, with a large button, of a shape frequently found in deposits of the earlier Iron age in this country. One extremity of the belt, it will be seen, ends in a very thin and narrow strap, which passing through the belt-loop, was twisted several times round the wooden sheath.

Metal *Mountings* for girdles were found in great numbers. Those of the types figured in Thorsbjerg, Plate 11, No. 49–51 and 53–55, are of rare occurrence. The fylfot ornament, *crux Gothica*, as it is sometimes called, occurring in Fig. 55, is highly characteristic of this period. About two hundred buckles and square girdle-ornaments—of shapes resembling those figured in No. 52 and 57–67 in Plate 11—were dug up in Thorsbjerg. The greater number are of bronze, plated with silver, occasionally also with gold, and variously ornamented, in the same way as other articles found in this deposit. The buckles of the forms 63 to 67 are, no doubt, of Gothic origin, the others we should be inclined to look upon as of Romanized style and work. How many square girdle-ornaments appertained to a complete set, I cannot determine. The highest number found of corresponding pieces was fourteen, and this number I think would suffice, with proportionate intervals, to ornament the belt the whole way round the waist.

---

[*] The eleven instances alluded to are the following:—1. An umbo of bronze (Plate 8, Fig. 16 and 16 *a*) and 2. A scabbard-tip of bronze (Plate 10, Fig. 41), both from Thorsbjerg. 3. An iron sword (Plate VII. Fig. 17 and 17 *a*), from Nydam; and 4. Several wooden shafts of arrows (Plate XIII. Fig. 36–39), from the same locality. 5. Silver mounting for a sheath (Worsaae's Antiquities, no. 381). 6. A bone comb; and 7. A wooden plane, covered with no less than eighty runes in five lines—all three from Vimose—the two last pieces found in 1865. 8. A fragment of a wooden shaft, represented in the accompanying woodcut; compare p. 22. 9. A golden diadem (*ibid.* no. 366), from Staarup, in Slesvig. 10. One  of the celebrated golden horns, from Gallehuus in South Jutland,—since stolen and melted down. 11. A bronze fibula (*ibid.* n. 384), from Baunshöi, near Himlingöie, in Sealand. Thirty-seven bracteates of gold, bearing inscriptions in these runes, are known, besides duplicates. Among our Runic stones there are nine, which, having regard to the form of characters on them, may be considered as belonging to a transition period. The author is indebted to Professor Stephens for these details.

The buckles from Nydam (Plate IX. Fig. 53 to 66) are of simpler work, and appear, on the whole, to be of Gothic origin.

We have, for the sake of convenience, considered all the buckles under this head, but it is scarcely necessary to point out that though the greater portion were adapted for belts, others may have had a different use, as, for instance, for harness.

### b. *Lances and Javelins.*

#### (Thorsbjerg, Plate 12, Fig. 1 to 4, and Nydam Plates X. and XI.)

Judging from the surprising numbers of wooden shafts and iron spear-heads found in our bogs, the spear must have been a common weapon among the people whose relics we are considering. In Thorsbjerg, however, nothing remained of the heads, except in the very few instances where they had been deposited wrapped up in chain-mail, in which cases small fragments were left. From these, however, we are not able to determine the usual form, but iron spear-heads of about the same period have been dug up in other Danish mosses, especially at Nydam, where they occurred in great number and variety.

The general form of the shaft will be better understood by reference to Plate 12, Fig. 1, and Plate X. Fig. 5, than by any description. It was mostly made of ash; the butt-end was rounded, and has never been furnished with a spike. The average length is about nine feet; the longest shaft was ten feet, the shortest eight feet; the diameter commonly one inch. On the middle of the shaft are often found either small bronze rivets between which a cord had been fastened, or a mounting of bronze; both of them probably for the purpose of indicating the point of balance for the weapon when

thrown, something like the amentum of the Greeks.[*] See Fig. 2, 3 and 4 in Plate 12, and the annexed che-mitype. The original, of which our illustration gives a fragment, is a complete shaft of the length of eight feet three inches; from the fracture in the middle there are forty inches and a half to the pointed end, and fifty-eight inches and a half to the butt-end; we may accordingly suppose that the iron spear-head must have had a weight equal to a piece of a wooden shaft of the length of about eighteen inches and a half.

[*] In a notice on the weapons of the Greeks in the 'Revue Archéologique' of 1862, N.S., vol. v. p. 175, M. Penguilly l'Haridon observes, " L'amentum . . . est une courroie placée à quelque distance du centre de gravité du javelot, et dans laquelle s'engagent les deux premiers doigts de la main droite. Quand on lance le trait, l'amentum fait à peu près l'office de la corde d'une fronde et augmente la force d'impulsion du bras de toute celle que peuvent fournir les doigts de la main." And afterwards: " L'amentum plié en deux, lié au bois par un nœud ordinaire, présente une ganse simple, où s'engagent les deux premiers doigts de la main dressée en l'air, la paume en dessus." See also the representation of a javelin with the amen-tum on a Panathenaic vase, with black figures, in the British Museum, given by M. Mérimée in the ' Revue Archéologique,' 1860, N. s. vol. ii. p. 211.

The principal varieties of form of the five to six hundred iron spear-heads from Nydam are the leaf-shaped, the bayonet-shaped, and the barbed. They vary in length from five inches and a half to twenty-three inches and a half, and have commonly a socket into which the pointed end of the wooden shaft was driven, and fastened with one or, in a very few cases, two or three rivets. Some specimens have flat tangs, to fit into the split end of the shaft (Plate XI., Fig. 30, 33, and 45). These are sometimes furnished with a ferrule at the junction of the spear-head with the shaft (Plate XI., Fig. 45, *a* and *b*). The rivets are commonly of iron, sometimes of bronze.

Most of the spears are devoid of ornament; but some specimens have points and stripes engraved in the metal, or a little round plate of gold let into the round part of the iron (Plate X., Fig. 9), or else a little wheel-shaped ornament of gold similarly inlaid (Plate XI., Fig. 40). Some of the first-named ornaments were perhaps grooves for the reception of gold or silver wire.

The spear-heads were often found in heaps, and, as it would appear, were originally deposited wrapped up in cloth, as was frequently found to have been the case in the Vimose deposit.

Before leaving the subject of the blades, I may mention that a wooden spear-head was found in Thorsbjerg, probably destined for the same use as the wooden sword mentioned at page 53.

The great length of these spears renders it probable that they have been used by horsemen rather than by foot soldiers, who at any rate would have great difficulty in wielding weapons of that length.

Under this head I shall also group—

### c. *The Awls,*

(Thorsbjerg, Plate 12, Fig. 5 to 8, and Nydam, Plate XV., Fig. 18 to 28,)

because they were chiefly used, I think, for the purpose of making a new hole when the thin spear-shaft had been broken immediately below the iron head, as must often have been the case. They have been part of the warrior's equipment, and the handles are accordingly perforated for the reception of a cord, by which the awl was worn suspended from his girdle in the same manner as the whetstones hereafter to be described. Fragments of bast-cords still remained in some holes. The handles are of wood or of bone, from two inches and a half to four inches and a half long, and sometimes very elegantly ornamented.

### d. *Bows and Arrows; Quivers.*

(Thorsbjerg, Plate 12, Fig. 9–11 and 15, and Nydam, Plates XII. and XIII.)

According to written testimony, bows and arrows were used by all ancient races, and the Goths, we are informed, made general use of these weapons for their infantry, though not for their cavalry. They used to commence the battle with missiles, and the Romans often suffered from their superiority in this mode of fighting (Procopius, and Gregory of Tours). Nevertheless the actual construction of ancient bows and arrows has hitherto been but little known, in consequence of their being made of such perishable materials, and the only remains preserved were arrow-heads of flint, bone, and bronze, mostly found in the graves of the Stone and Bronze periods. Nor indeed could we expect to find iron arrow-heads in the graves of the Iron age, on account of the oxidation of the metal.

The wooden *long-bow*, which was held vertically by the middle in the left hand, is uniformly straight, thicker in the middle, and of decreasing thickness towards the ends. The common length is about five feet; different sections are given in the Plates. The bows have at both ends crossed bands of thread to fasten the string, or else notches in the wood for the same purpose. They are generally flat on the inner side and convex on the outer, the edges being a little rounded. No less than forty bows of this description were found in Nydam; some were discovered in the boat, and about fifteen lay together. It is to be observed that two of them had spikes, one of iron, the other of bone (Plate XII., Fig. 10 and 15), so that in case of need these bows may have been used as spears. In Thorsbjerg bows occurred less frequently, only three specimens having been found, but these had elegantly-engraved designs on the. outer side ; the various carved ornaments are shown in Plate 12, Fig. 9 *a*, 9 *b*, and 10 *a*.

*Arrow-shafts* occurred frequently in both places, as frequently almost as javelins, sometimes in bundles of twenty or thirty. They exhibit all the same elegant form as represented in Plate 12, Fig. 11 and 11 *a*; they are from two feet three inches to three feet long; the diameter of a section in the middle is shown in full size, Fig. 11 *b*. One end is pointed and cleft for the reception of the tang of the head, or, in very rare instances, merely pointed so as to fit into the hollow socket of an arrow-head. The other end shows where narrow bands and thread were twisted round it, in order, perhaps, to secure four rows of feathers, of which, however, no portions remained. The shafts found in Nydam are remarkable on account of the frequent occurrence upon them of different signs (represented in Plate XIII.), which may have served as the owners' marks. The victors could thus after battle collect the proofs of their successful valour, and not be deprived by others of the honour of their deeds. As an illustration, we are reminded of the arrow which the Danish King Sven Tveskjæg sent round among his guests, at the festival in commemoration of his father's death, and which was acknowledged by Palnatoke as belonging to him.

As all arrow-heads, which were probably of iron, were wanting in one of these peat-bogs, it was a happy circumstance that great numbers of them were preserved in the other, for though the two deposits cannot be regarded as quite contemporary, we may be justified in combining the general forms of objects from one of these deposits with those of the supplementary remains found in the other, and thus obtaining a complete idea of the weapons of the time.

The one hundred and seventy specimens of arrow-heads of iron and of bone brought to light in the diggings in Nydam, present different forms, of which the leaf-shaped, the four-sided, the three-sided, and the barbed, are the most common. Their length is between two inches and a half and six inches, and ornaments are rarely found upon them. (Plate XII., Fig. 5, 6, and 18–32.)

Nydam moss is the only peat-deposit which has yielded *quivers*. One of them was of wood and richly decorated. (Plate XIII., Fig. 63.) Of the other, only the bronze fittings seem to have been deposited (Plate XIII., Fig. 64), as no traces of the quiver itself were left.*

Whilst the spears, on account of their length, as already stated, must have been ill adapted for warriors on foot, and therefore, as well as the small shields of about two feet in diameter, most likely were used by the cavalry,—bows and arrows, we think, belonged to the infantry; swords, no doubt, were common to both.

### e. *Whetstones,*

(Thorsbjerg, Plate 12, Fig. 12, and Nydam, Plate XIII., Fig. 65–69.)

most probably used for sharpening smaller weapons and instruments, such as arrow-heads and awls, occur frequently in almost all deposits of this period, and the systematic excavations brought forth no less than about one hundred specimens. They are small oblong stones, with traces on the broad side of their use for sharpening, and either left in their natural shapes, or with a groove worked round them for the reception of a cord by which they have been carried hanging from the girdle. A few square stones of a soft substance are also known from these deposits. (Plate XIII., Fig. 67.)

---

### 7. HARNESS.

(Thorsbjerg, Plates 13 to 16, and Nydam, Plate XIV.)

A great number of bridles, bits, and other portions of horse-trappings, a driving-rein, and fragments of waggons, prove abundantly that the people of the Early Iron age had a full knowledge of the use of the horse; they had trained the animal to their service, and understood how to ride it as well as to use it for draught. The beauty of the bridles and of the

* A bronze end-socket of a quiver (see the accompanying woodcut) was found along with other objects near a skeleton in a gravel-pit by Aasoe, in Sealand. We have undoubtedly similar specimens preserved in the bronze objects represented in Plate 15, nos. 42 and 141, of Neville's 'Saxon Obsequies,' London, 1852, and there described as boxes.

I 2

various metal fittings of the harness, and the surprising metallurgic skill evinced in them, will convince us of the advanced state of civilization in this respect in the Early Iron age.  It will be seen by the following description, that much care was employed in the manufacture and ornamentation of horse-trappings, and that precious metals were often used for their decoration.  Many of the articles, however, which we now consider as necessary for the horse and rider, were then unknown.  Stirrups, saddles, and horse-shoes came later into use; the earliest known specimens seem to belong to the last period of heathenism, between the sixth and tenth centuries.

The Goths, according to ancient writers, made good cavalry soldiers, and we are told that Justinian the First, during a war, purchased horses of them.  To procure provender for their horses, they chose for their place of assembly a town surrounded by extended plains. (Procopius, de Bello Goth.)  These statements, it is true, apply to a somewhat later time, when the Romans had come into close contact with the Goths on the frontiers of the Empire, and afterwards in Italy, but they hold good also as regards an earlier part of their history.  Horses are frequently mentioned, and the names of the horses of the gods are cited, in our earliest mythological poem, the Older Edda.  It was a favourite animal with one of the gods, and when Baldur died, his horse was led on to his funeral pile.

The only tolerably well-preserved *head-stall* which is left from antiquity was found in Thorsbjerg, and represented in Plate 13, Fig. 1, some details being drawn full-size in No. 1a to 1d.  It is almost complete, and in all essential points wonderfully like some of those used nowadays.  It is made of stout leather, ornamented with bronze studs, of which the heads are silver-plated.  The drawing shows the ordinary triangular openings for the horse's ears formed by the head, the front and the crown strap in the middle.  A large stud indicates the place where we fix the rosette, and beyond this crossing point the continuation of the front forms a throat-lash, whilst that of the head forms the head-pieces on each side, in which the snaffle-ring is suspended by means of hooks passing through slits in the lower ends of the head-pieces.  To the snaffle-rings are attached, besides the hooks for the head-pieces, the bridle, which consists of flat rings joined by solid links of bronze; a strap, of which only a fragment was left, but which no doubt was a lip-strap, taking the place of the chain, and finally a bronze case for the reception of the bit, which must have been of iron, but which is now destroyed.  All the other pieces of metal are of bronze.  The crown-strap is continued beyond the front into a large face-piece, by which an ornamental plate of bronze was suspended, which in the head-stall in question is only a fragment, but of which perfect specimens are represented in Plate 15, No. 26–31.  To the sides of this plate, which protected the nose of the horse, smaller straps were evidently attached, which were tied behind the lower jaw of the horse, or perhaps to the snaffle-rings, thus performing the office of the nose-strap, and keeping the plate in its place.  If this supposition be correct, it will be seen that not a single necessary piece was wanting, and that the harness makers of those times thoroughly understood the principles of their art.   The two large transverse straps at the top of the drawing evidently descended one on each side of the horse's neck; but the use of them cannot be determined with certainty.

Besides this complete set, a great many single pieces were discovered in Thorsbjerg, whilst only a very few were found at Nydam, where they all lay near skeletons of horses.

Of *bits* we found only one at Thorsbjerg, which was of bronze (see the accompanying figure).   But six iron bits with snaffle-rings were discovered at Nydam, three of them between the jaws of horses' skulls.

Bronze.   ⅓.

Several bronze *bridles* and fragments of one similarly shaped, but of iron, were dug up at Thorsbjerg.   Some terminate in square metal pieces, ornamented on the outside, and with remains of a leather coating inside (perhaps remains of a leather middle-piece for the hand; see the drawing of the complete head-stall).

Three pairs of *snaffle-rings* with cheek-plates and mountings attached for head-pieces and leather bridles, but without trace of the bit, were found at Thorsbjerg. (See Plate 14, No. 12, 13, 14.)

Several *nose-pieces* destined to protect the horse's nose, are represented on Plate 15, Fig. 26–31; they are purely characteristic of the Thorsbjerg and the Vingsted deposits, none like them having to my knowledge been found elsewhere.  They are certainly not Roman, and must be regarded as affording a special instance of "barbarian" contrivance.

A very great number of ornamental *studs* and *bosses* for placing along the leather straps, as may be seen in our figure of the complete headstall, and in representations of such objects on Roman sculptures of the first centuries after Christ.   They occur in a great variety of shapes, figured in Plate 13, Fig. 2–11.

A still greater number (about two hundred) of a very peculiar kind served probably for *fringe-like ornaments* for the edges of leather straps, of which remains were discovered on their cleft ends.   (See the Profiles 42 *a* and 43 *a* on Plate 15.)   Their principal varieties are represented on Plate 15, Fig. 36–48, and Plate XIV., Fig. 6–11.

One bronze *spur* only was found in Thorsbjerg (Plate 15, Fig. 32 and 32 *a*) among so many other objects belonging to harness.   It is not complete, as the conical spike which we know from other contemporary specimens (compare pp. 12 and 15) to have belonged to it, is now wanting; being probably of iron, it has corroded.   In Nydam we found several iron spikes like the original of Plate XIV., Fig. 5, which may probably have belonged to spurs.

Of doubtful use, but certainly appertaining to harness, are the following objects from Thorsbjerg:—

1. Four bronze objects; like that shown in Thorsbjerg, Plate 14, Fig. 22 and 22 *a*.

2. The pendant, Plate 14, Fig. 23, which ought perhaps to have been drawn in an inverted position. It somewhat resèmbles a very large spur, and this kind is of rare occurrence in Denmark; in Ireland, however, they are frequently found in somewhat similar forms; and Sir W. R. Wilde* is of opinion that they may "have been slung from the rings of the bridle-bit, or were attached beneath the horse's jowl. In the latter position," he observes, "they could only serve as ornaments; in the former, they would prevent the horse from grazing."

3. The bronze object represented by Fig. 16, 16 *a*, and 16 *b*, in Plate 18. At the time when the plates were being engraved I could not determine its use. Afterwards I saw in the Copenhagen Museum a similar piece, found near Ebeltoft, in North Jutland, proving that whatever its use may have been, it belonged in some manner to a bridle.

Along with all these antiquities from Thorsbjerg were dug up some remains of waggons, the principal of which was a fragment of an oak *wheel*, (see Fig. 2 in Thorsbjerg, Plate 16,) much like those of the present day, and composed of several smaller pieces held together by strong wooden pegs or dowels. The projecting ends of the spikes served to protect the felloe, so that the rim has not been furnished with any metal tire. Judging from the fragment preserved, the wheel was little less than three feet in diameter. The original of Plate 16, Fig. 3, I take to have been one-half of a *splinter bar*. Some large pieces of wood, which may also have belonged to a chariot, were unfortunately so incomplete when taken up, that no definite idea of their use could be formed.

Here may also be mentioned a complete *driving-rein* (Fig. 1 in Plate 16), ten feet six inches long, formed of three leather straps joined together by small bronze rings. The complex leather straps figured within the rein were found together with it, but we cannot make out for what purpose they were intended.

---

## 8. AGRICULTURAL IMPLEMENTS.

### (Thorsbjerg, Plate 16, and Nydam, Plate XV.)

1. A scythe blade from Nydam (Plate XV., Fig. 17), about fifteen inches long, was so much corroded that its exact form could not be ascertained, nor its breadth determined. Similar objects are known in their perfect state from Vimose on Fyen, and from La Tène, in Lake Neufchâtel.†

* In his 'Descriptive Catalogue,' Dublin, 1861, p. 608-9.

† See Keller, 'Pfahlbauten,' 2ter Bericht, Zürich, 1858; and Desor, 'L'Age du Fer dans les Constructions du Lac de Neufchâtel' (' Musée Neuchâtelois,' Sept. 1864).

2. Wooden harrows and rakes were found at Thorsbjerg (Plate 16, Fig. 4), one of which is about seven feet long, although the shaft is not complete. The latter is roughly hewn, square, and terminating in a pointed end to be passed through the transverse piece, which is furnished with wooden teeth about nine inches long. Some shafts have perforated holes to receive a cord by which to draw them, for they are so clumsy and heavy that one man could not manage them.

3. Several tethering-poles of neat workmanship, with a deep notch in the upper end, and between five and fifteen inches long, were also discovered at Thorsbjerg.

## 9. OBJECTS OF DOMESTIC USE.

### (Thorsbjerg, Plates 16, 17, and Nydam, Plates XIV., XV.)

The deposits contained a large number of *household vessels* both of clay and of wood, spread over the whole area; but the water had decomposed some, and the superincumbent layers of peat had broken many to pieces, so that comparatively few remained in such a state of preservation that the forms could be ascertained. The clay of which some are made is mingled with pulverized quartz. We draw particular attention to the clay vessel represented in Plate XIV., Fig. 22, because of its evidently common parentage with many pieces of pottery found in German and Old English graves.* A few similar vessels have been found in burial places in Slesvig. The sizes and forms of the other vessels are various—large cooking-vessels, household pottery of ordinary sizes, platters, cups, and goblets. Almost all were, as I have already stated, discovered a little beneath the layer of antiquities; many were sunk by means of large stones, and in the handles of some were found remains of cords. In one instance, a wooden vessel was found inside an earthen pot; another was discovered in a basket of wicker-work, and two of the earthen vessels contained half of a hauberk of chain-mail rolled up and including fragments of small iron objects, such as spear-heads, knives, etc. The largest cooking-vessels had marks of fire at the bottom, and were about sixteen inches high. Examples of the ordinary household pottery are given in Plate 17, Fig. 21 to 23; they are of the average height of four inches and a half. The most elegant, though a very common form, is represented by Fig. 10–12; some of these vessels—the original of Fig. 10, for instance—are so symmetrical in shape, that there is good reason to believe they were turned on a lathe, while all the others seem to be hand-made. These also afford the oldest known examples of a black vitrified glaze, and are formed of a finer clay than other specimens. Other forms, but of more rare

* Kemble on Urns from Stade-on-the-Elbe, in 'Horæ Ferales.' London, 1863.

occurrence, are seen in the small cups or goblets, Fig. 13, 18, 19, and 24, of rough workmanship. The original of Fig. 20, it would appear, is a crucible.

On the whole they are devoid of ornament, and where such is found, the figures have been roughly and carelessly engraved on the moist clay. (See Fig. 14 to 17, and 19.) The originals of 10 *a* and 11 are exceptions, the handle and the ornaments being more carefully executed. The fylfot ornament on the bottom of a vessel (Fig. 11 *a*) deserves attention.

The wooden vessels—Plate 17, Fig. 1 to 8—are usually of elegant forms and well finished. So far as we can judge from the original of Fig. 1, a block of wood was first roughly chopped into shape, and then turned on a lathe. Wooden vessels have been found in the four mosses, in which systematic diggings have been made, and they apparently formed the finer and more elegant household vessels of the Iron age. Besides these, we have from the Nydam find a large and thick water-trough, roughly hewn (Plate XIV., Fig. 25), and staves of a wooden pail (Fig. 24) ten inches and a half high, with traces of metal hoops. It would seem also that barrels have been deposited in this place, for the original of the annexed figure is certainly a stopper for a wooden barrel.

Fig. 6. Plate 17, represents a little *wooden box* with a cover. I cannot indicate its use, but several similar specimens were discovered in Nydam. (Plate XIV., Fig. 15–17.)

Fragments of *baskets* of wicker-work were of frequent occurrence ; the pattern in which they were usually plaited will be seen in Plate 16, Fig. 12.

The *axes* of this period are of two different kinds, as repre-          ½.    Wood.
sented by Plate XV., Fig. 10 and 13. The latter is of the kind commonly called " celts." These socketed celts of iron have been discovered not only in Nydam, but also in Vimose, though the shaft in the last-named locality was somewhat different. Both sorts of axes were implements of domestic use, we suppose, and not martial weapons.

In both places wooden *clubs* were brought to light ; but those from Thorsbjerg were on the whole finer and more elegant than the specimens found in Nydam. (Compare Plate 16, Fig. 5, 9, and 10, with Fig. 15 and 16 in Plate XV.) Some of these clubs are made out of one piece of wood ; in other cases, the heads are of a harder wood than the handles.

I cannot determine the exact use of the original of the annexed figure. It may possibly have been used as a sort of crowbar.          ½.    Iron.

Under the head of domestic objects, we have also to mention *knives* and *spoons* (Plate 16, Fig. 11, 15–17, and Plate XV., Fig. 2–9). At Thorsbjerg only the handles of the knives were left, and they are smaller and more elegant than those from Nydam. The last-mentioned find contained eighty-six specimens of knives, of which many were well preserved and complete, between six and thirteen inches long, with broad backs, and, in a single instance, the blade was hollow-ground. The handles are usually made of a hard sort of wood, and unornamented. Only one handle of solid brass was found.

The piece represented by Fig. 1 in Plate XV. is supposed to have been a *sheath* for a knife. It is roughly cut out of wood and has a groove round the top, in which there are remains of cords. It was found beneath the fir boat.

Another article which was also discovered near the fir boat may have served as a *fishing-net*. It is formed of cord, and fastened to a piece of wood of a singular shape (Plate XIV., Fig. 14).

There were found, moreover, twelve pieces of *pyrites* (Plate 16, Fig. 13) for striking fire. Steels for that purpose are not yet known as belonging to this period.

*Knotted and plaited fabrics, cords, and strings of bast* were frequently met with over the whole extent of the diggings. For the most part they were the remains, we may suppose, of the cords by which the objects had been tied together.

Whether some of the wooden originals represented by Nos. 23 to 34 in Plate 18, belonged to a *loom*, I cannot positively say, though I think it probable. They were found separately, and are incomplete. I refer for further particulars to the engravings and to the description of the Plates.

Some arched pieces of wood, of which the commonest form is represented in Plate 16, Fig. 14, seem to have answered as *stretchers* for suspending slaughtered cattle. These were found only in Thorsbjerg moss.

---

### 10. RING-MONEY AND ROMAN COIN.

(Nydam, Plate XVI., Fig. 20–25, and the Vignette on the title-page.)

It has been often surmised that foreign trade was very active during the Bronze age, and some have even maintained that the bronze objects used in northern countries were imported from the south. Yet not a single instance is known in Denmark of coins of any description having been discovered along with relics characteristic of that period. It is in the Early Iron age that foreign coin and ring-money make their first appearance. During this period smaller and larger fragments of bracelets and other personal decorations were used as a metallic currency to replace or supplement the direct interchange of commodities. Our earliest native coins are of the eleventh century (King Sven Tveskjæg). At first they appear to have been rare; and barter, it is believed, was carried on until the time of Sven Estridsen (1046–1076).

The ring-money found here comprises:—

K

1. Fragments of golden Bracelets, six of them forming parts of one and the same bracelet. (See page 42.)

2. Golden Rings, linked together in twos and threes. Originally they may perhaps have been finger-rings; at the time of their being deposited they were clearly used as ring money. (See Plate 16, Fig. 25.)

Under this class we may group some Touchstones, one of which is perforated. (See Fig. 18 and 19 in Plate 16.)

The thirty-seven Roman silver denarii found in Thorsbjerg (the earliest and the latest are represented on the title-page) extend over the period from 60 to 194 after Christ. They are of the following Emperors and Empresses:—

Nero (1), Vitellius (1), Vespasian (4), Domitian (1), Trajan (7—one of these is an ancient counterfeit, being copper plated with silver), Hadrian (6—one counterfeit), Ælius (1), Antoninus Pius (6—one counterfeit), Faustina the Elder (1), Marcus Aurelius (3), Faustina the Younger (2), Commodus (3), and Septimius Severus (1).

The last, as I have stated above, was minted A.D. 194. The coins are mostly much worn, and a few have marks of fire upon them.

In Nydam, Roman denarii were discovered, embracing about the same period as those from the other moss, 69 to 217 of our era, and of the following Emperors and Empresses:—Vitellius (1), Hadrian (1), Antoninus Pius (10), Faustina the Elder (4), Marcus Aurelius (7), Faustina the Younger (1), Lucius Verus (2), Lucilla (2), Commodus (5), and Macrinus (1). The latest of these coins was minted in the year A.D. 217[*]

*They give us an approximate date for the objects with which they were found. Allowing some time for their transport from southern countries, the deposits in our peat-bogs cannot have taken place before about the middle of the third century.*

All the known coins from discoveries of this age—from mosses, graves, and chance finds—are of the three first centuries of the Christian era; the latest known is of Macrinus (A.D. 217). Among them, coins of the Antonines are of most frequent occurrence.

---

## 11. OBJECTS OF UNKNOWN USE.

### (Thorsbjerg, Plate 18.)

I have often had occasion to observe that the objects from both our moss depositories were mostly found incomplete; partly because they had been so when they were first buried, and partly on account of the decomposition of the iron. It was, moreover, the first time that antiquarian excavations of such an extent had been undertaken,

---

[*] Obv.: Laureate head. IMP(erator) C(aius) M(arcus) OPEL(ius) SEV(erus) MACRINVS AVG(ustus). Rev.: PONT(ifex) MAX(imus) TR(ibunitia) P(otestate) CO(n)S(ul) P(ater) P(atriæ). Jupiter standing, a spear in his left hand, and the thunderbolt in his right.

and the use of many of the objects dug out in a fragmentary condition had for the first time to be explained and determined. By degrees, as more perfect or better-preserved objects were brought to light, especially in the Nydam find, it became possible to arrange many of the previously indeterminate fragments under the different classes,

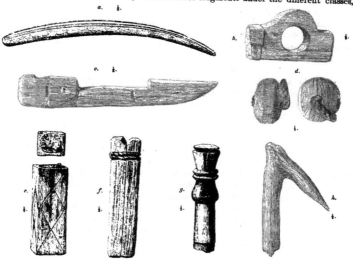

which we have now been considering. Still too many objects remain unclassified. A description of these would be of little use; I must refer the reader to the engravings in Plate 18,* to the Index to the Plates, and the annexed figures representing some of the seemingly more important nondescript objects from the Nydam depository. They are all of wood; the original of Fig. f consists of two pieces roughly cut, and tied together by means of a cord.

---

## 12. HUMAN AND ANIMAL REMAINS.

Portions of human skeletons have certainly now and then been discovered in our peat-mosses, containing antiquities of the Early Iron age, but hitherto not in such a

* The portion of a bridle (Fig. 16), the fragments of umbones (Fig. 17 and 18), mentioned at pages 61 and 49 respectively, must be excepted. Fig. 19 to 21 are studs for sandals, etc.

juxtaposition with the other relics as would justify us in pronouncing them undoubtedly contemporaneous.  There exists, for instance, a communication dated in 1809, from a clergyman in Snogbæk, near Nydam moss, stating that human bones had been found in this moss together with iron arms; as, however, these bones have disappeared, we cannot be sure that they really were human, especially as no human skeletons or even bones have been found during the systematic diggings either in the two South Jutland mosses or in Kragehul moss in Fyen.  A skull of a child and a fragment of another skull were discovered in Vimose in 1865, but not in very close connection with the antiquities, and in places where these lay only sparingly scattered.  They were found exactly at that depth at which the antiquities ceased, and until other discoveries afford more certain information, it remains impossible to decide whether they belong to the race of the Early Iron age or even are contemporaneous with the antiquities.

Bones of horses and other animals are, on the contrary, not unfrequently found in these mosses, though the case is different as regards each of the four which have hitherto been thoroughly examined.  In those of Thorsbjerg and Kragehul (Fyen) but few bones were met with; in the former they were found in cutting peat, and we have no information as to whether they occurred together with antiquities and at the same depth; in Kragehul so small a part of the moss was left for systematic investigation, that the bones discovered, which, moreover, have not yet been properly examined, were too few to allow of any well-founded conclusion.  In the third antiquarian moss which has been systematically excavated, viz. Vimose, in Fyen, near Broby and Allesö, the layer of antiquities was, as it were, sown over with bones almost exclusively of horses, mixed with and surrounded by the antiquities in such a manner that their association could not possibly be ascribed to accident.  I have more than once heard it suggested that they were the remains of old worn-out horses which had been killed from time to time by a blow with an axe on the forehead, and then thrown down into the peat trench near which they had been executed.  But although many of the skulls certainly exhibited a rather large hole in the forehead with splintered edges, yet, considering that many were found with antiquities lying under and over them, in large heaps splintered and hewn to pieces, and close to chopping-blocks with many marks of extensive use, it seems more reasonable to consider them as forming part of the deposit.  I must, however, observe, that the osseous remains from Vimose have not yet been examined by any physiologist.

With regard to the bones found at Nydam, no doubt can exist as to their having really formed part of the original deposit.  They were scarcely so numerous as in Vimose, and less scattered over the whole area; whether this is due to the bones having got into the moss at Nydam in another manner than at Vimose, or to the motion of the water in the latter place having spread them more equally over the space occupied by the antiquities, I cannot say.

Skeletons and parts of skeletons were found at Nydam on the shell-strewn bottom, and often surrounded by antiquities below, above, and on the sides. Near a tolerably complete skeleton of a horse were found, besides shield-boards, shafts of lances and other wooden objects, several beads, two iron bits, several metal mountings for shields, an iron spear-head, a whetstone, several arrow-heads, an awl of iron, and a Roman silver denarius. Not far from it were two skulls and other remains of horses, and near them some iron bits. The skulls of horses, which, just as those last mentioned, appeared to have been deposited without the other parts of the animals, had still their bits in their mouths, one of the bits being incomplete and evidently deposited in that state. And if there could still be any doubt as to the skeletons being contemporaneous with the antiquities, it must yield to the fact that several of the skulls have been exposed to a similarly violent and inexplicable ill-treatment as the vast majority of the other objects deposited. (Compare, for instance, the cut-up boards of a boat, Plate IV., Fig. 27, and page 29.) All the bones in Nydam were of horses, excepting a skull and some other fragments of one of the smaller races of oxen. In the mouth of this skull there was a board of a shield, a circumstance which, however, probably was due merely to the accidental movement of the water.

Several boxes with bones from Nydam were forwarded to the Museum of Natural History at the Copenhagen University, for the inspection of the learned director of that institution, Professor Steenstrup, who has been good enough to communicate to me his observations on these skeletons, from which the following extracts may be found interesting:—

Professor Steenstrup remarks, first of all, that the three skulls which he has had under inspection are those of three stallions, aged respectively about three, six, and ten or eleven years. The length from the condyloid processes to the anterior edges of the front teeth is from 49 to 50 centimetres, and the stallions were consequently of middle size. There is an almost complete skeleton belonging to the oldest of these three skulls, and the horse has probably come into the moss, if not in an entire state, at any rate as an almost complete skeleton. Of the two stallions, no other bones were found besides the skulls except those of the four extremities, the two forelegs from the forearm to the hoof-bone, and the hind-legs from the stifle-joint downwards. Professor Steenstrup lays stress on this remarkable difference between the three individuals in the number of bones preserved, as the two, of which only the skulls and the lower parts of the extremities have been found, cannot of course have perished on the spot, or the other parts of the skeletons would have been discovered in the same place. With regard to this point the learned Professor states, that he has several times found skulls not only of horses, but also of oxen and sheep, either alone or together with the lower parts of the four limbs, in such positions in the peat, that there could be no doubt but that they had been purposely immersed in the water, where the peat afterwards formed itself round them. In those cases, however, the limbs were cut off below the knee and hock, marks of the cutting instrument being often distinctly traceable, whilst no such marks

have been discovered on the horse bones from Nydam as could indicate a severance
of the limbs, or that the flesh had been eaten.

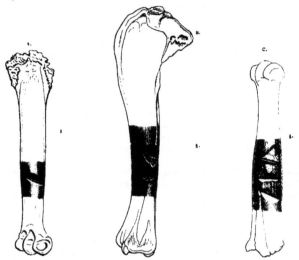

    With regard to the third tolerably complete skeleton, two circumstances are parti-
cularly noticed by Professor Steenstrup.   One is, that those bones which were found
with the antiquities bear unmistakable evidence of some carnivorous animal—wolves or
large dogs—having had access to them before their immersion in the peat, just as is
the case with innumerable other bones from other peat-mosses.   At the same time,
the marks of teeth on the bones from Nydam are so few, and confined only to those
parts which are usually attacked first, that the carnivorous animals cannot be supposed
to have had access to them for any length of time, nor can the bones have been long
exposed to the air before they were buried.
    The other fact commented upon by Professor Steenstrup is the existence of
extensive and very distinct marks of sword-cuts (Fig. A, B, and C).   A minutely-splin-
tered fracture has been produced by the chip having been broken away from the bone
by a vigorous twist of the sword, leaving a smooth, sharply-cut surface; and this
circumstance seems to indicate that these violent blows have been inflicted when the
bones were no longer covered by flesh; for, if the flesh had still been on the bones,
these would probably have presented a more jagged or roughly splintered fracture.

Similar incisions with sharp swords are observable on all three stallions' skulls; and on two of them they are both deep and numerous. The second skull (Fig. D) is the worst treated of the three. It shows not less than ten different cuts, of which six are in a transverse direction across the forehead between the upper part of the nose and the top of the head, whilst four are found on the right side of the face, the bones of which have been cut through. Several of them are ten or thirteen centimetres long, and the direction of the cuts—all more or less across the skull—seems also to indicate that the person who inflicted the blows had the horse's head lying on the ground before him. The oldest of the skulls has had six heavy blows not less deep than those of the preceding. Their depth and direction is shown in Fig. E.

D.

E.

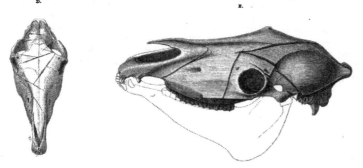

The manner in which these bones have been treated must necessarily be considered in connection with the violent ill-treatment to which the numerous weapons and ornaments have been subjected. Professor Steenstrup cannot believe that the bones could have been cut in battle in the manner described while the animal was living. If the horses were killed in battle, he thinks that this ill-treatment must have been inflicted afterwards. He regrets that he has not succeeded in finding on any of the bones examined by him such crossings of cuts of swords and marks of the teeth of carnivorous animals, as would show more clearly which were first inflicted; but the circumstance that all the lower jaws are entirely free from cuts inevitably suggests the idea that the lower jaw had already fallen from the head when this received the heavy blows. It had certainly separated from the skull when the wolf gnawed the articular processes of one of them.

Besides this, there are evident traces of these stallions having been exposed to a shower of arrows. One of them has got one of the four-sided arrow-heads deeply fixed in the upper part of the posterior margin of the left shoulder, whereby precisely such a sharply-defined quadrangular hole has been produced (Fig. F) as may be observed in many of the shields and bucklers; one of the ribs of the same horse has a three-cornered hole, caused by a pointed missile. In both holes, which still contained rust,

F.

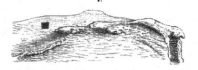

the iron points have been fixed till the bones were taken out of the peat, when they have either fallen out or crumbled away, being probably reduced to rust at the time.

Professor Steenstrup observes in conclusion, that the oldest of these stallions has not presented a handsome figure while still living. Its teeth were very irregular; it was very badly spavined, and its back very much broken. "To do justice to the equipment of warriors in those times," Professor Steenstrup concludes, "I will assume it to have been a baggage horse."

# APPENDIX.

Professor L. R. von Fellenberg, in Bern, has, in ' Berner Mittheilungen,' nos. 497–8 and 535–6, given the following results of analyses of some of the objects from Thorsbjerg presented to him by M. A. Morlot, of Lausanne :—   .

| | Copper, per cent. | Zinc, per cent. | Tin, per cent. | Lead, per cent. | Iron, per cent. | Silver, per cent. | Nickel, per cent. |
|---|---|---|---|---|---|---|---|
| Roman bronze helmet (Fig. 1, Plate 5) | 82·98 | 6·56 | 9·77 | 0·51 | 0·18 | | |
| Umbo . . . . . | 96·12 | | 2·41 | 0·21 | 1·16 | 0·10 | |
| Rim of an umbo .  . | 90·19 | 4·92 | 3·41 | 0·90 | 0·20 | 0·38 | |
| Upper part of an umbo, similar to Plate 8, Fig. 13  . | 93·67 | 4·17 | 1·96 | 0·10 | 0·08 | 0·02 | |
| Handle of a sh eld  . | 98·42 | | 1·26 | | 0·23 | | 0·09 |
| Different fittings  . | 87·54 | 5·72 | 4·98 | 1·51 | 0·22 | 0·03 | |
| Bosses or studs similar to Plate 18, Fig. 19–21 . . . | 89·33 | 3·18 | 6·84 | 0·50 | 0·07 | 0·08 | |
| Small nails. . . . | 25·00 | | 10·44 | 12·83 | 0·24 | 51·49 | |

L

# INDEX TO THE PLATES.

———◆———

## PLATES I.—IV.

### BOATS FROM NYDAM. (Pp. 29–39.)

PLATE I.—Clinker-built oak boat, seen from different points.

PLATE II.—Measurements and details of construction of the oak boat: the measurements are given in English feet (see the scale). 1 and 2. Plan and side view of about one-half of the boat. 3–7. Sections at the 10th, 14th, and 18th ribs, and near the prow, showing the shape of the ribs and their position with regard to the clamps˞on the boards, to which they were tied by cords passed through the holes in both. 5 *a*. Section of the gunwale board. 5 *b*. Section of the bottom plank, and the boards on either side of it. 6 shows the construction of a thwart; 7, the section of the sternpost; 8 shows the connection of the prow and the bottom plank. 9 *a, b,* and *c*. Side-rudder; the handle at the top can be detached.

PLATE III.—Details of the oak boat. 10. Interior view of one end of the boat. 11. A clamp of the upper row supporting the heads of the ribs; in the holes are remains of cords. 12. One of the ordinary clamps; 13. Fragment of one of the oak boards, with iron nails. 14. Part of the two top planks, seen from the inside. 15–18. Rowlocks of deal. 19–20. Oars of oak and of deal. 21–22. Ends of long deal poles roughly hewn; the original of 21 is twenty feet eight inches, that of 22 about fourteen feet long; two such poles were found in the oak boat, two others in the fir boat. 23. Round wooden spar about three feet long, with a hole at each end; several bundles of twenty to thirty similar spars were found in the spaces between the ribs of the boat, and they have, no doubt, belonged to the boat's inventory (stretchers?).

PLATE IV.—24–25. Rowlocks of the fir boat of which the remains are described, pp. 35–37. 26. Wooden instruments of unknown use with rounded perforated ends, frequently found in both the boats; from forty to sixty inches long. 27. Fragments of an oak board with projecting clamps, which are ornamented in some places, and rowlocks, not made from separate pieces, but cut out of the same piece with the gunwale board, p. 29. 28. Portion of a wooden conduit; on one of its sides the figure of an animal is rudely engraved. 29. The middle thwart of the large oak boat (comp. Plate II. 6). 30. In oak, found in the boat, but of unknown use and incomplete. 31–32. Pieces of wood destined for repairs in the fir boat. 33. Ornamented figure (of a bird?) found in the oak boat. 34. Small thwart for one of the ends of the boat. 35–36. Wooden scoops.

## WEARING APPAREL. (Pp. 40, 41.)

(Thorsbjerg) PLATE 1.—Kirtle of woollen cloth. *a*, shows the woven pattern in the sleeves; *b*, the border below; *c*, the loose wrist-band.

(Thorsbjerg) PLATE 2.—1. Trowsers of woollen cloth. 2. The pattern. 3. Pattern of the stockings. 4. Pattern of a woollen cloak, p. 40. 5. Pattern of another woollen cloak.

(Thorsbjerg) PLATE 3.—Leather sandals, p. 40. 1. Unfolded sandal for the left foot. 2. Fragment with a border of silvered bronze rivets; 2 *a* has probably belonged to the same sandal. 3. Fragment, with an impressed ornament.

## PERSONAL DECORATIONS, ARTICLES OF THE TOILET, ETC. (Pp. 41–43.)

(Thorsbjerg) PLATE 4.—1–13. Fibulæ, bow-shaped and circular, all of bronze. [Fig. 4, 6, and 7 are covered with silver gilt plates.] 14. Bulla in gold. 14 *a*. Piece of the rim, actual size. 15. Pendant of gold (for an earring?), actual size. 16. Bronze finger-ring. 17–24. Beads, the larger ones perhaps buttons: (17, 18, and 19, of glass; 20, of agate; 21, of greenish glass; 22 and 23, of variegated porcelain; 24, of white glass, with a gold-foil within.) 25–26. Tweezers of bronze. 27. Die of amber, p. 43.

(Nydam) PLATE V.—1–2. Silver clasps, one of them set with two pieces of blue glass. 3–8. Tweezers and ear-picks; 4 and 6 of silver, the others of bronze. 5. A silver double box, p. 43. 9–11. Combs of bone. 12–14. Bronze fibulæ. 15–17. Pendants of bronze and silver in the shape of small weights (p. 42, and compare Fig. 3 in Plate 18). 18–22. Beads and buttons, made of coloured glass, except Fig. 21 and 22, which are of amber. The originals of 23–27 were found together, and have apparently belonged to the same piece (helmet? see p. 44); 23 is of wood the others of bronze plated with silver and gold.

## DEFENSIVE WEAPONS.

### HELMETS. (Pp. 43–45.)

(Thorsbjerg) PLATE 5.—1. Neck-piece of a Roman helmet in bronze; the designs are embossed in the thin metal. 1 *a*. Piece of the arched top-piece. 2. Bronze serpent, of Roman workmanship; it probably once ornamented a helmet. 3. Silver helmet, of Gothic origin, in many places covered with ornamental gold plates. 4. Front view of the crown or head-piece. Compare also the bowed plate in Plate 11, 47 (p. 45), and perhaps Pl. V., 23–27.

### CHAIN-ARMOUR. (Pp. 46–48.)

(Thorsbjerg) PLATES 6 and 7; all the figures actual size.—1. Breast-plate in bronze, plated with silver and gold. [*b*, side view; *a*, one of the heads in open-work; *c*, *d*, and *e*, three of the figures of animals which have been riveted to the breast-plate at a later time, but did not originally belong to it.]   2 and 3. Patterns of interlinked chain-mail.   4 to 6. Buckles for hauberks: 4, in bronze with silver-gilt plates—the designs are embossed; 5, of iron; 6, of bronze.  7. Breast-plate, formed in the same manner as Fig. 1; the Medusa-heads are struck from the same die as those on Fig. 1; the outer rim is a mixture of Barbarian and Roman workmanship: whether it originally belonged to the piece is doubtful (7 a, the profile; 7 b, one of the Medusa-heads).  8. Richly ornamented bronze buckle, with platings of gold and silver; the reverse, with iron rings still attached to it, is shown in 8 a, side view of the central part in 8 b.

### SHIELDS. (Pp. 48–52.)

(Thorsbjerg) PLATE 8.—1. Circular wooden shield, composed of nine boards.  2 and 3. The greatest and smallest thickness of the boards.  4. The central opening, with recess to hold the handle.  5–10. Handles: 5, in wood; 6, of wood fastened to the shield with wooden pegs, and with its bronze covering fastened with bronze rivets; 7–9, of bronze; 10, in silver, with two golden transverse bands.  11–18. Umbones: 11, in thick bronze, with a Roman inscription, shown full-size in 11 c; 11 b, thickness of the metal; 11 a, side-view; 12, in thick bronze, and apparently of Roman workmanship; 13 and 14, of thin bronze and Gothic manufacture; 15, inner coating of wicker-work for a thin metal umbo; 16, fragment of thin bronze of the shape of either 13 or 14, with a Runic inscription,—shown full-size in 16 a; 17, of bronze,—it is badly mutilated at the top; 18, fragment of thin silver, with embossed golden ornaments on the outer rim, and figures of animals and other ornaments cut out from golden plates and laid on the piece, one-half the actual size; 18a, one of the outer ornaments, full size; 19–22 and 32, rims of bronze in various shapes and sizes; 21 a and 22 a, seen from the end; 23 and 23 a are the front and back of a fragment of a wooden shield repaired with bronze plates.  24. Wooden fragment repaired by means of bronze clamps.  25–31. Bronze pieces of various shapes and sizes, intended for repairs or ornaments on wooden shields.  32: see 19.

### OFFENSIVE WEAPONS.

### SWORDS. (Pp. 52–56.)

(Nydam) PLATE VI.—DAMASCENED SWORDS OF IRON.—1. Ornamented with lines on each side, and with triangular bronze pommel.  3. Ground hollow: on the tang are two makers' stamps: it had a handle of wood similar to that represented by 2 in Plate 9, but which has not been preserved.  3. The handle is of wood, with silver platings.  4. Handle of bone, in three pieces.  6. Upper part of a bone handle with bronze mounting.  7. Wooden handle, with round pieces of ornamented bronze.  8. Of massive bronze.  9–11. Patterns of damascened sword-blades.

(Nydam) PLATE VII.—12. Damascened; with two longitudinal hollows; the section shown in 12 a.  13. Not damascened.  14. Forged in facets; the maker's mark is shown full size at the side of the figure; it occurs on either side of the blade.  15. Damascened; the section shown in 15a.  16. Damascened; the original has in one edge twenty-three marks of sharp cuts, eleven in the other.  17. Not damascened; the figures inlaid in the blade with flat gold wire are shown full size in 17a.  18. Damascened; below the name, RICVS, on the grip there is maker's stamp.  19. Damascened; the Latin number XX. is engraved on the tang; 19 a, section of blade.  20–21 (both damascened) and 22 (not damascened) have Latin stamps, p. 53. On 22 there is a second stamp like a crescent, with three horns behind it. The sword, of which a fragment is represented in 22, is thirty-four inches long, and one inch and three-quarters broad; the length of the grip is four inches and three-quarters.

(Thorsbjerg) PLATE 9, 1–19.—SWORD HILTS.—1. Complete hilt of wood, with plaited bronze bands covering the handle proper, bronze rivets ornamenting the two end-pieces, and a small bronze knob at top; 1a, the lower end-piece from below. 2. Wooden handle without any ornament; this species was of frequent occurrence. 3. Fragment of a rudely-made wooden sword. 4. Wooden handle, of unique shape, roughly made; 4a, the same, seen from below, full-size, to show the difference from 1a, which was obviously intended for a two-edged sword. 5. Hilt of wood, with ornamented silver bands, of rare occurrence in this deposit, but not unfrequently met with in the moss of Nydam. 6 and 6a are hollow pieces of thin silver, once forming parts of a handle like 5; on 6 the fylfot ornament is engraved in a complex manner, showing that though the sign may have had originally a symbolical meaning, it is here only an ornament. 7. Button-shaped pommel of bronze, of very frequent occurrence. 8 and 9. Pommels of wood, ornamented with large and small silvered rivets. 10. Of silvered bronze, ornamented as shown in 10a. 10b. Fragment of a hilt with golden ornaments, and probably belonging to 10. 11–19. Pommels of hilts like Fig. 1, of wood, partly with ornaments cut in the material, partly ornamented with bronze rivets in various designs. 20–28. Chapes of bronze, except Fig. 25, which is in silver: in 23 and 27, remains of the wooden scabbard are left.

(Thorsbjerg) PLATE 10.—SHEATHS.—29. Fragment of a triangular wooden sheath with bronze mounting, of a kind frequently occurring in contemporaneous deposits. 30. Bronze rim for the upper part of a wooden scabbard; in the squares are plates of silver, gilt and ornamented. 31. Complete wooden scabbard, with elegant bronze fittings: it is obviously of Romanized workmanship, but hitherto unique among our antiquities. 31a. Mouth of the same. 32. Silver rim with fragments of a wooden sheath. 33–40 (and 43). Metal loops for suspending the sword on the belt: 33, bronze with gold and silver ornaments; 34, of thin silver; 35, bronze with transverse bands of ornamented silver plated with gold; 36, of bronze; in the bird's head ornament are marks of arrow-heads; 37, of bronze covered all over with silver and gold, and very elegantly ornamented with various designs; 38, of bronze still fastened on the fragment of a wooden sheath of plain work, and such as frequently occur in the larger moss deposits; 39, of bronze with engraved ornaments inlaid with silver; 40, bronze with ornamental transverse bands of silver and gold; above and below are rows of triangular grooves, destined for the reception of a substance now lost, perhaps silver; 40a, side-view; 43, plain mounting of bronze. 41. Bronze chape, with clear and distinct Runic inscriptions on both sides: 41a, showing the letters on the reverse; 42, of bronze with ornamented rosettes in silver gilt. 43 (see after 40). 44–46. Fragments of wooden sheaths: 44 has a bronze chape; 45 is ornamented with lines carved in the wood; 46, it would appear, has had no metal mounting; it is here shown from the inner side; 46a gives the thickness of the wood.

(Nydam) PLATE VIII.—SHEATHS.—23–24. Rims for the upper part of sheath, bronze. Fig. 25, wooden sheath with a bronze fitting, shown full-size in 25a: this sheath was discovered in its present incomplete state on the iron sword represented by Plate VII., Fig. 22. 26–27. Wooden sheaths. 28–36. Scabbard-fittings; all of bronze except 32, which is made of bone. 37–39. Scabbard-tips of bronze. A raised ornament is carved on the piece of wooden sheath represented in 39. 40–43. Belt-loops of bronze, except 41, which is of iron.

(Nydam) PLATE IX. 44–50. Scabbard-tips.  44 is of iron; the patterns are of flat gold wire inlaid in the iron.  45–50 of bronze.  46 and 47 are cut and pierced in several places, and in such a manner as could hardly have occurred in battle.  51–52. Bronze studs.  53–66. Buckles, all of bronze, except 59, which is of iron, and 62, the bow of which is of solid silver.

(Thorsbjerg) PLATE 11.—Shoulder-belt, Buckles, and other Metal Mountings for Belts, etc., except 47, the original of which may have belonged to a barbarian helmet, see page 45.  48. Shoulder-belt of thick leather ; in the middle is a large bronze button, shown also in 48a and 48b. One end is broad and emarginated with a button hole ; to the other end a triangular piece is sown on, terminating in a long leathern tongue, which was intended to be passed through the eye formed by the metal mounting on the middle of the sheath and twisted several times round the latter.  49–51 and 53–56.  Bronze fittings for shoulder-belts ; most of them plated with silver and gold, and ornamented in different ways ; 55 has the fylfot ornament in open work.  52 and 57–67.  Buckles and square plates for sword-belts, all in bronze.  (57 is plated with silver and ornamented with gold plates ; 63–67 are obviously not Roman.)

## SPEARS, LANCES, JAVELINS, AND AWLS. (Pp. 56, 57.)

(Nydam) PLATE X.—1–4 and 7–21, leaf-shaped lance-heads ; on 1, 4, 8, and 9 are ornaments engraved in the iron, possibly intended to receive gold or silver wire.  16, with octagonal socket, 18, with faceted ridge, and 21, with flutings on either side of the ridge, recalling certain Irish bronze spears, are very rare forms in our finds.  5. Complete javelin, with the casting cord round the middle ; ten feet four inches long.  6. Fragment of a wooden shaft, with projecting nails in it, and wound round with string.

(Nydam) PLATE XI.—22–38. Barbed iron spear-heads, some much bent.  39–45. Bayonet-shaped spear-heads.  They have usually a hollow socket, polygonal, round, or lozenge-shaped, but some, as 30, 33 and 45, are tanged to fit into a split shaft, in which they were secured by a metal ring ; 46, is a bronze ring for this purpose.  The illustrations, 30, 30a, 45a and b, show the details of this method of fixing the head.  22, 31, 33–36, and 43, present forms of rare occurrence. The ornament on 40 is inlaid with gold.

(Thorsbjerg) PLATE 12.—1–8 and 16, lances and awls.  1. Perfect shaft of a lance, nine feet six inches long, made of ash ; both the ends and the middle are shown one-half the actual size. 2. Middle part of a lance shaft, with remains of a cord.  3. Fragment of a shaft with bronze rivets.  4. Fragment of a spear shaft with a silver mounting.  16. Bronze ring for a spear-shaft. Compare Nydam, Plate XI., 45 and 46.  5–8. Wooden handles for awls, some perforated for suspension ; 6a shows the top, 8a the bottom of one of these handles, with the socket for the awl. (See below, Nydam XV., 18–28.)

## BOWS AND ARROWS, QUIVERS, AND SHARPENING STONES. (Pp. 57–59.)

(Thorsbjerg) PLATE 12 continued.—9–11. Bows and arrows.  9. Bow of yew with ornaments carved on it, and traces of the cords that have held the string.  9a and 9b. Piece of the bow, actual size ; 9c, section of the middle.  10. Fragment of a wooden bow, with carved and punctured ornaments.  The fragment was found in the condition shown by the drawing.  10a. Piece of the bow full-size, to show the details of the ornamentation.  10b. Section.  11a and b. Arrow-shaft of deal, with notch for the bow-string, wound round with string possibly for fixing four rows of feathers, and split at the upper end to receive the tang of an iron head which was secured with string. 12. Oval whetstone with traces of wear, and a groove running round it, probably for a string by which to carry it. 15. Fragment perhaps of a bow; 15a, side view; 15b, section.

13. Iron axe, with wooden handle to be passed from above through the opening in the head. 13a. Another specimen seen from above. 14. Ornamented wooden handles. (See below, Nydam, Plate XV. 10.)

(Nydam) PLATE XII.—1-9. Details of wooden arrow-shafts; the heads on 5 and 6 are of iron, the shaft itself is roughly pointed on 1 and 4. The complete arrow, represented by 5, is two feet nine inches long. On 7, 8, and 9, ornaments are carved at the notched end. 10-17. Long bows of wood. 10 has an octagonal spike of horn; 12 is ornamented with longitudinal lines engraved in the wood (see the section and the figure at the side); 12a represents the end. 15 has an iron spike. 16 has a notch for the string and a projecting bronze nail. 17 is wound over with pitchy thread. 18-32. Arrow-heads of bone (18-23) and of iron (24-32).

(Nydam) PLATE XIII.—33-62. Parts of arrow-shafts, on which are engraved owner's marks and Runic letters (35-38, and also, perhaps, on 39-41). 63. Quiver of wood, closed at one end by a massive wooden stopper. 63b, 64, and 64a. Bronze mounting for a quiver; no traces of the woodwork remained; in the engrailed edge of the mouthpiece and end socket are small nails with silver-plated heads. 65-69. Whetstones: 67 is of a rare form.

## HORSE HARNESS AND RIDING AND DRIVING GEAR. (Pp. 59-62.)

(Nydam) PLATE XIV.—Fig. 1-13. Riding gear. 1. Bit, consisting of two bronze rings of unequal size and a middle-piece of iron. 2. Twisted iron bit. 3. Bit of iron fixed in bronze sockets, with bronze rings jointed. 4. Iron bit. 5, of iron, is supposed to have been the spike of a spur. 6-11. Pendants of bronze, except 8, which is of silver. 12, 13. Bronze rings, with loose bronze fittings. (For continuation of this Plate see below.)

(Thorsbjerg) PLATE 13.—1. Complete head-stall of leather; the heads of the bronze rivets—serving as rosettes—are covered with ornamented silver plates: the bridle is composed of bronze rings. 1a. Bronze cap for the bit proper. 1b. Bronze hook for the head-piece. 1c. Bronze ring of the bridle, side view. 1d. Thickness of the leather straps. All the figures full size. 2-11. Rosettes of bronze for fastening together the leather straps; 4 is of silver, plated with gold on the fluted knob; 11 is bronze plated with silver, with fylfot ornaments.

(Thorsbjerg) PLATE 14.—12-14. Cheek-plates of bronze: 14 is plated with silver. 15-25. Bronze bridles and mountings. The square end-pieces in 18 and 19 are covered with ornamented plates of silver and gold. Pieces like 20 may also have belonged to sword-belts.

(Thorsbjerg) PLATE 15.—26-31. Bronze pendants for protecting the nose of the horse. (Compare Plate 13, 1.) 29 and 30 are overlaid with silver and gold plates. 32. Fragment of a bronze spur; the spike is wanting. 33-48. Pendulous ornaments; perhaps for a sort of fringe to the bridles; in bronze, except 35, 36, and 40, which are in silver. (Comp. Plate XIV., 6-11.)

(Thorsbjerg) PLATE 16.—1. Driving-rein, page 62. The bit, which was probably of iron, is now wanting, though the bronze end-caps remain. In the middle are figured some leather straps, with buckles and rings of bronze of uncertain use. Compare page 61, and the bronze bit there figured. 2. Fragment of an oaken wheel, page 62. 2a. Section. 3. Fragment of an oak splinter-bar (?).

AGRICULTURAL AND DOMESTIC IMPLEMENTS, RING-MONEY, TOUCHSTONES.
(Pp. 62–66.)

(Thorsbjerg) PLATE 16 *continued.*—4. Wooden rake; the teeth are about nine inches long, p. 63. 5. Complete wooden club or mallet; the head is of a harder wood than the shaft. Heads of somewhat different forms are given in 9 and 10. 6. Wooden wedge. 7. The pointed edge of a long wooden pole. 8. Fragment probably of an axe-handle (see Nydam, Plate XV., Fig. 14). 11. Bowl of a wooden spoon; fragment. 12. Pattern of the wicker-work in a basket enclosing a wooden vessel, p. 63. 13. Piece of pyrites. 14. Wooden stretcher, p. 65. 15–17. Handles of knives: 15 is in solid brass, 16 and 17 in wood. 18–19. Touchstones: the original of No. 19 is perforated, p. 65. 20–25. Ring-money in gold, one-half the actual size, p. 65; compare the golden bracelet figured in p. 42. The three rings (25) were found linked together.

(Nydam) PLATE XIV. *continued.*—14. Part, probably, of a fishing net; the cords are fastened to a web of bast bands, and this again fastened to a wooden pole. 15–17. Small wooden boxes without lids. Compare Thorsbjerg, Plate 17, 6. 18–21. Wooden vessels and cups, turned on a lathe. 22. Vessel of clay, with projecting massive knobs. The impressions round the neck of the vessel, 23, were produced by a finger when the clay was wet. 24. Six staves of a wooden bucket, with marks on the wood of four iron hoops. 25. Large wooden trough.

(Thorsbjerg) PLATE 17.—Household vessels, pp. 63–64. 1–6 are of wood. 1. Roughly chopped out. 2. Unfinished. 6. Vessel with cover. 7–24. Cooking vessels, household vessels, cups, platters, etc., of burnt clay. 10 *a* shows the handle of 10. 11 *a* shows the bottom of 11, with the fylfot ornament. Fig. 20 may be a crucible.

(Nydam) PLATE XV.—Objects of domestic use. Fig. 1. Roughly-cut cylinder of wood, possibly a knife-sheath. 2–9. Knives with iron blades and wooden handles. The ornaments on the backs of 4 and 7—a rounded notch on either side, with rows of sharp notches across the back of the knife, above and below—are highly characteristic of our Early Iron age. 10–14. Axes, of the two forms known of this period, p. 64. (See Thorsbjerg, Plate 12, 13 and 13*a*.) 15. Large club, made of rather soft wood. 16. Wooden mallet? of a single piece. 17. Iron blade of a scythe, much corroded. 18–28. Awls. The handles, 18–21, are of bone, and very elegantly turned on a lathe; the other handles are made of wood. 25 is furnished with an iron ring, instead of the hole which is usually found in the handles of these implements (s. Thorsbjerg Plate 12, 5–8).

(Thorsbjerg) PLATE 18.—OBJECTS OF UNKNOWN USE (p. 66), except the following:—6, a bronze button. 12. Probably fragment of a buckle (plated with gold and silver). 16. Probably belonging to harness (see p. 62), in bronze. 17 and 18, which latter ought to have been drawn in an inverted position, are fragments of shield bosses, both in bronze; 17 is solid, 18 hollow (compare p. 50); and 19–21, buttons of bronze and of silver, actual size; of very frequent occurrence in this deposit. The use of the other articles has not been determined: 1 in silver, 2 bronze, 3 bronze filled with wood (pendant or weight?—compare Nydam, Plate V., 15 and 17, and page 42, 7); 4, bronze, plated with silver; 5, bronze; 7, 8, and 10, bronze, plated with precious metals; 9, bronze; 11, bronze; 13, thin silver band, with raised stripes; 14–15, bronze, plated with silver; 22, bronze; 23–34, of wood.

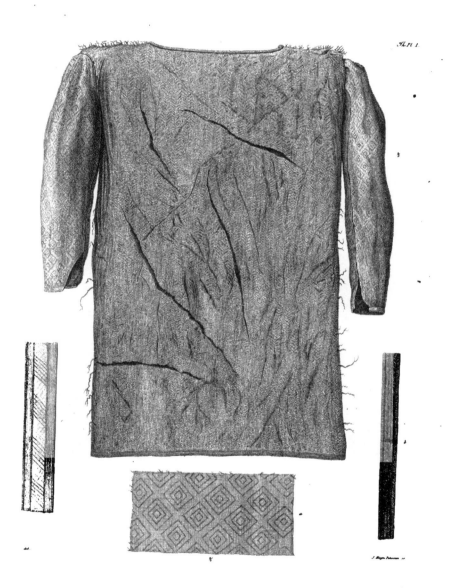

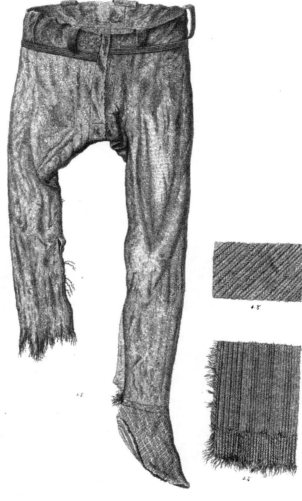

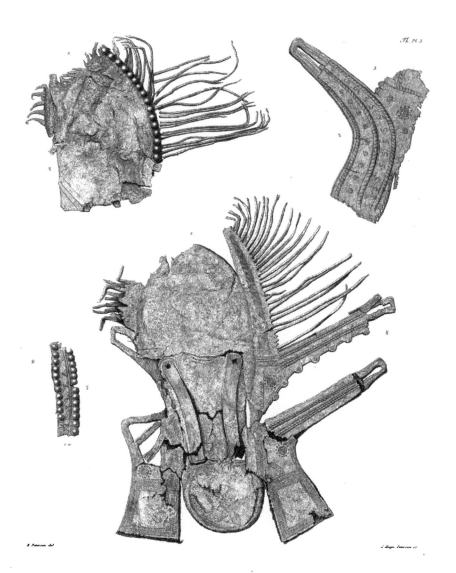

B. Petersen del.

J. Magn. Petersen sc.

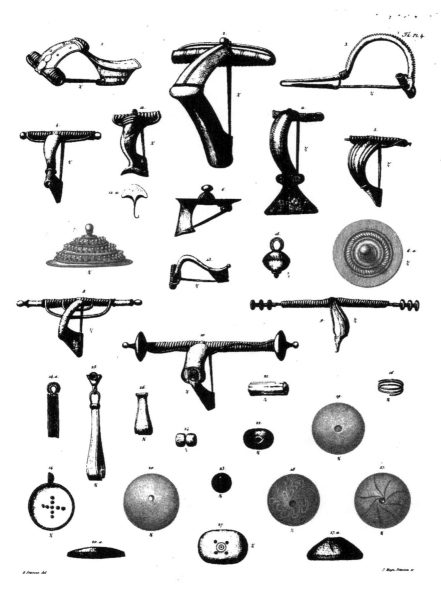

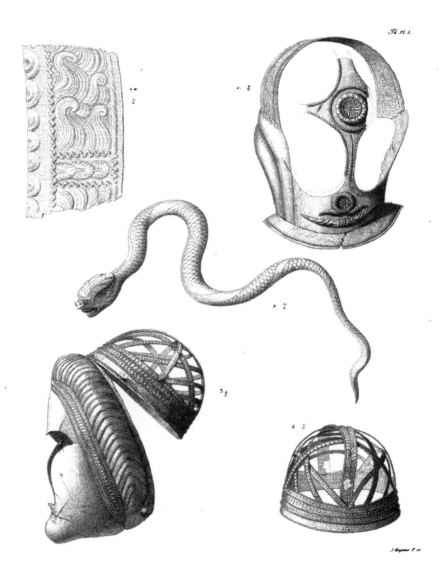

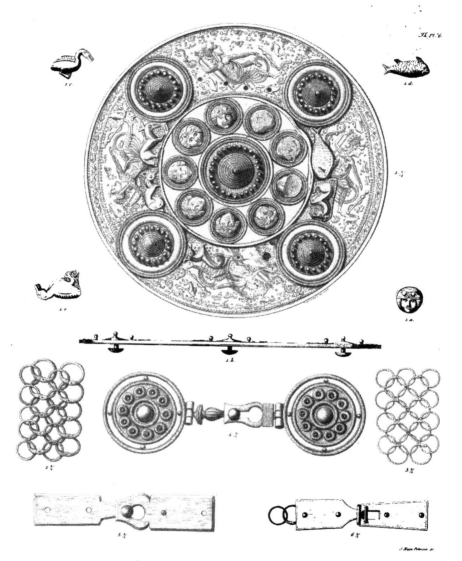

J. Mayr Petersen sc.

Tab. 17.

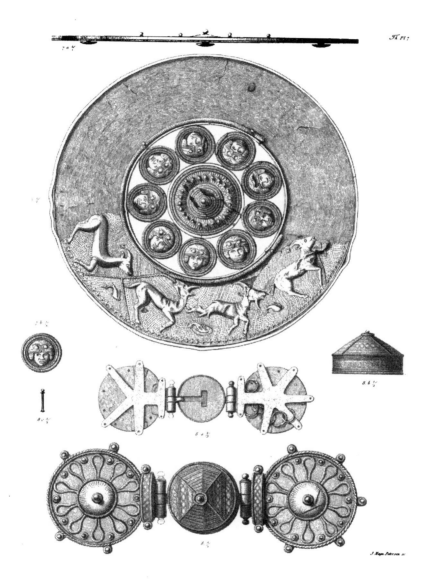

J. Magn. Petersen sc.

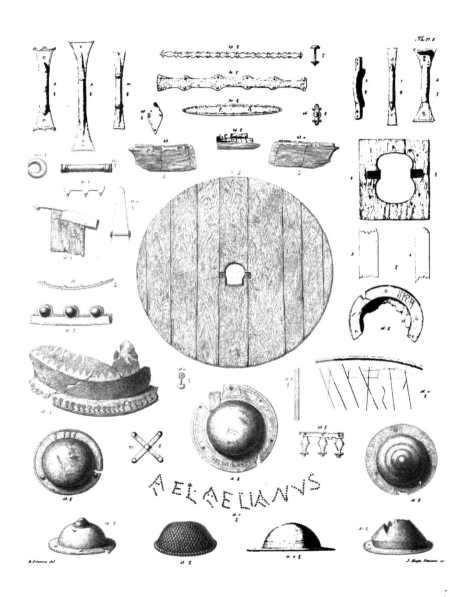

AEL AELIANVS

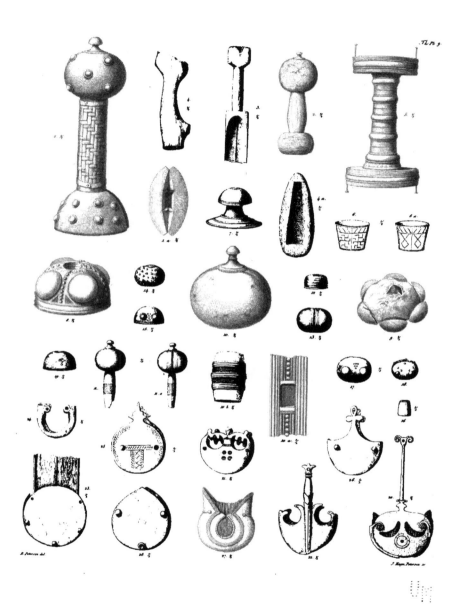

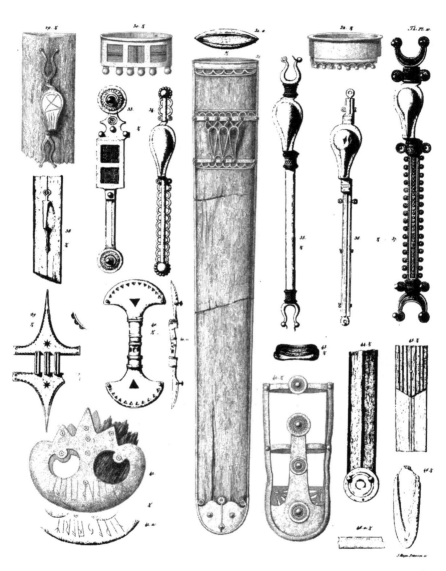

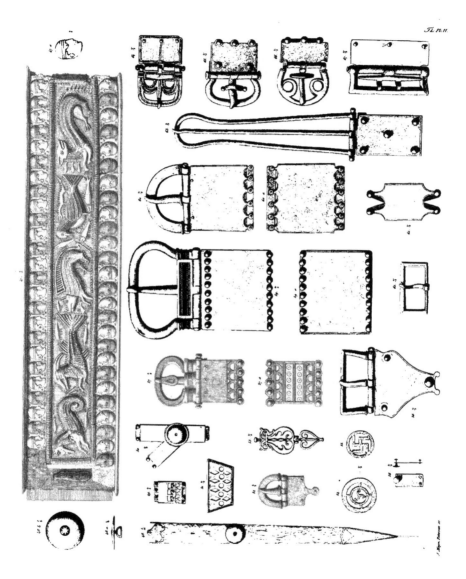

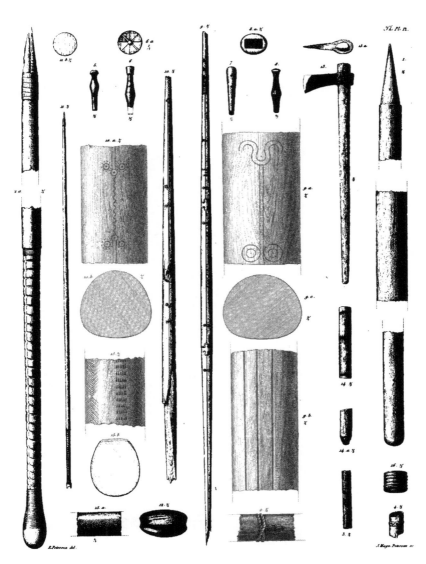

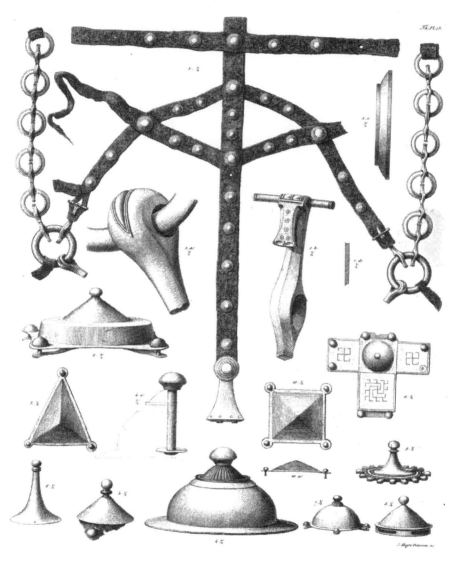

J. Mayer Peterson. sc.

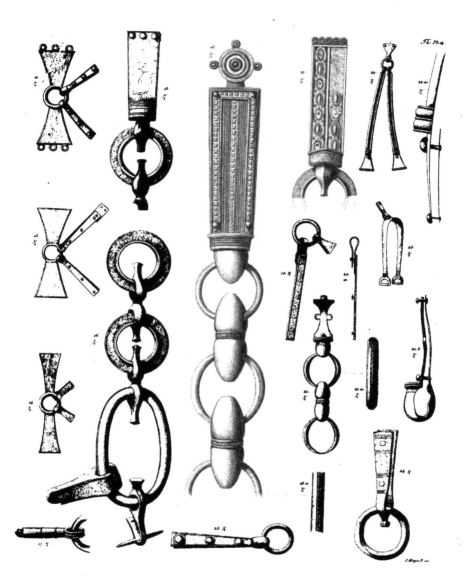

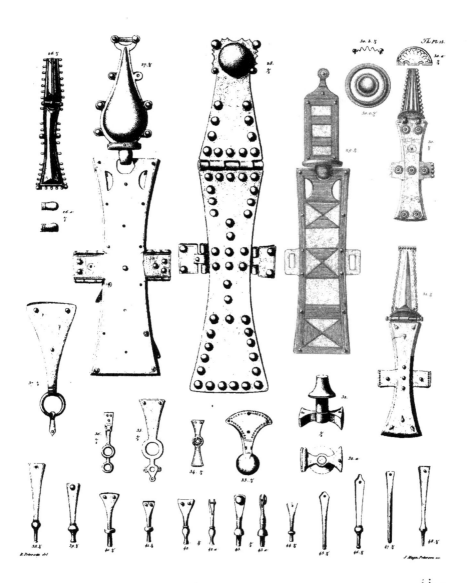

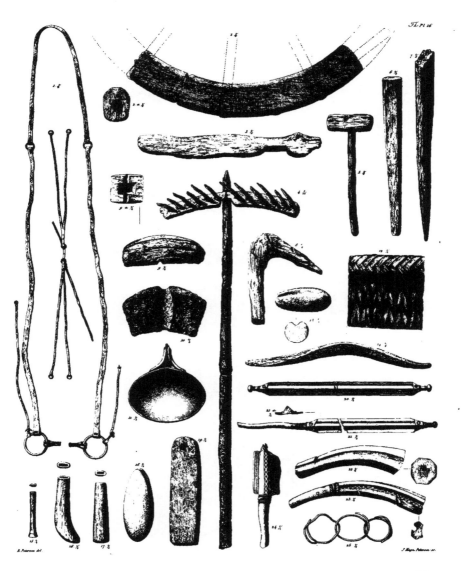

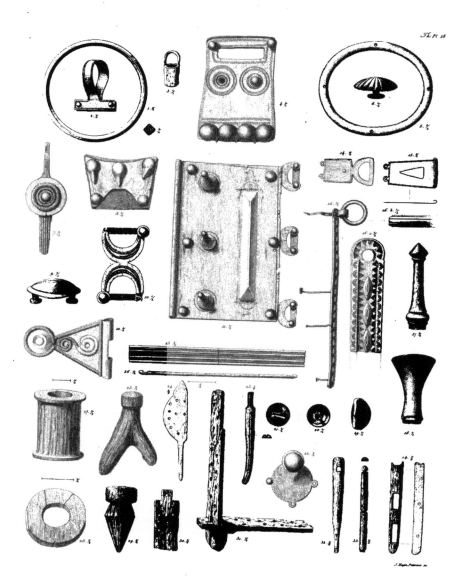

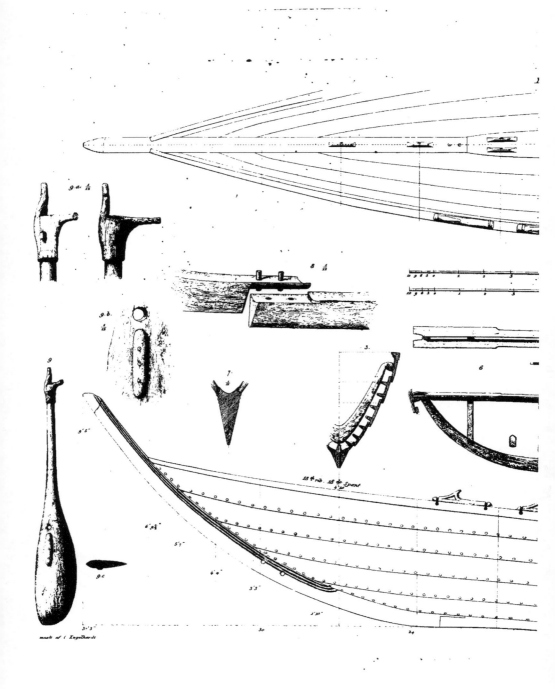

9 a. $\frac{4}{15}$

9 b. $\frac{4}{15}$

9

9'5"

6'9½"

5'7"

4'6"

3'5"

1'10"

9.c

7 $\frac{4}{15}$

8 $\frac{4}{15}$

3.

6

15 de rib. 15 de Spant
5'2"

3'5"

30

34

masts of ( Engelhardt )

2

1

10 English Feet

10 Fod

5.a. $\frac{1}{8}$

4

5.

Ved 10de Spant:
at the 10th rib

5.b. $\frac{1}{8}$

1.

14th rib
14de Spant

10th rib
10de Spant

18                    11                    6

Magnus Petersen sc.

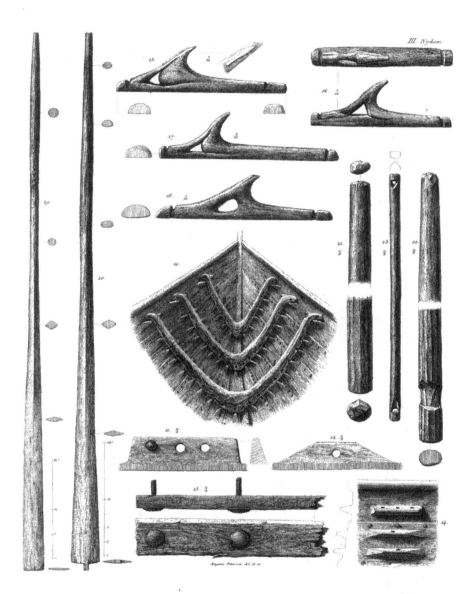

Magnus Petersen, del. & sc.

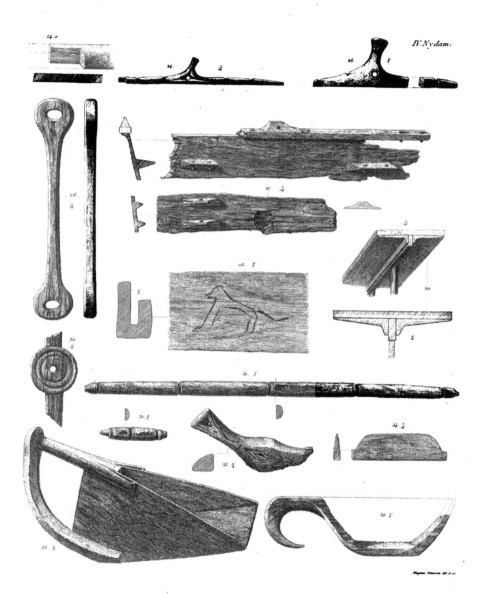

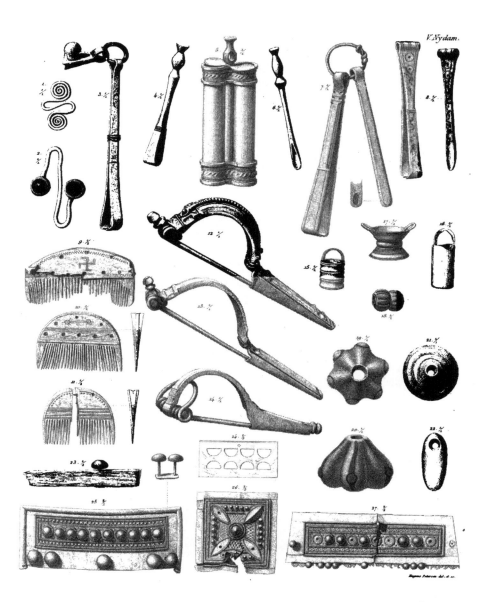

V. Nydam.

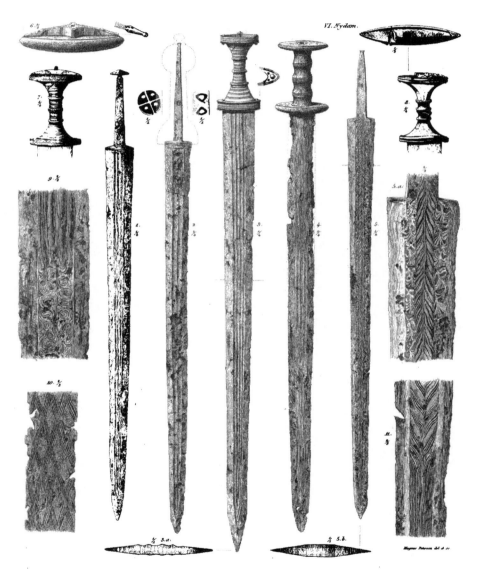

Magnus Petersen del. & sc.

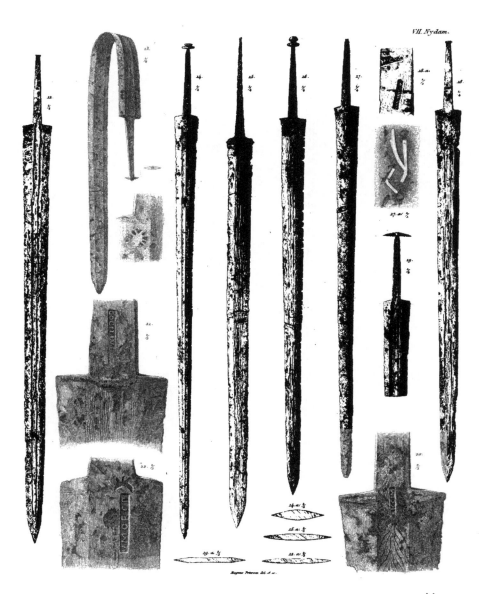

*Magnus Petersen del. d. w.*

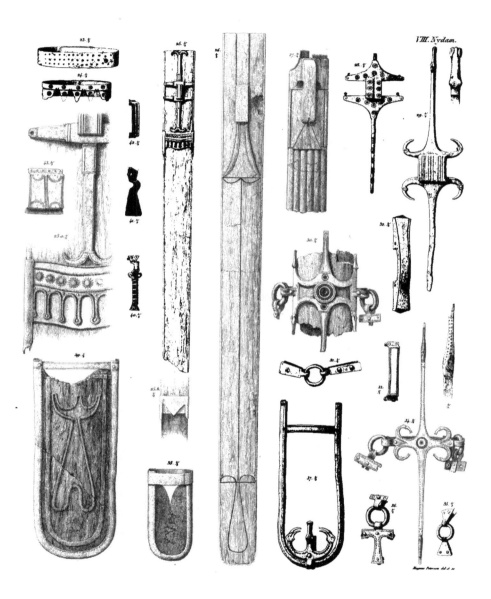

VIII. Nydam.

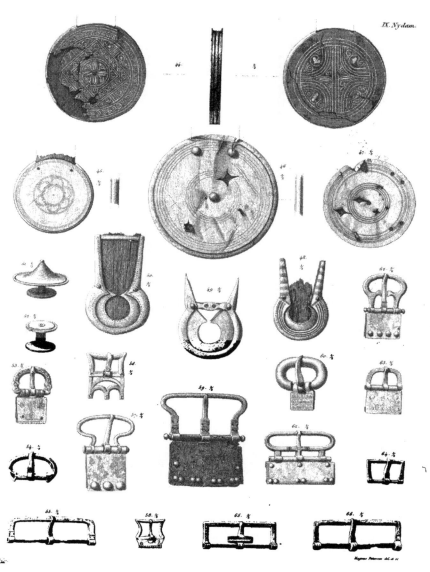

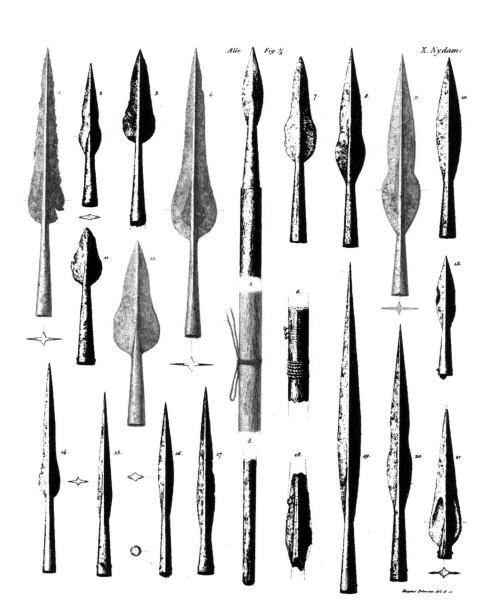

*Alle Fig. ⅓*      *X. Nydam.*

*Magnus Petersen del. d. sc.*

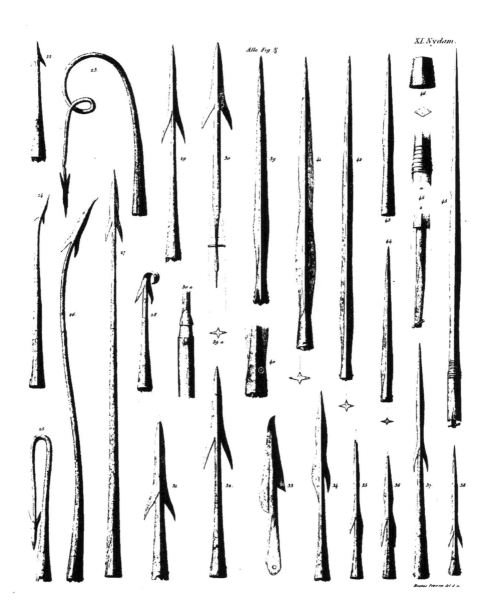

Alle Fig ⅔

XI. Nydam.

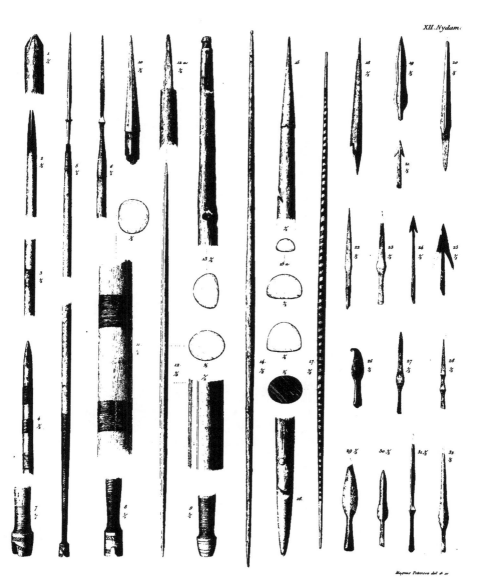

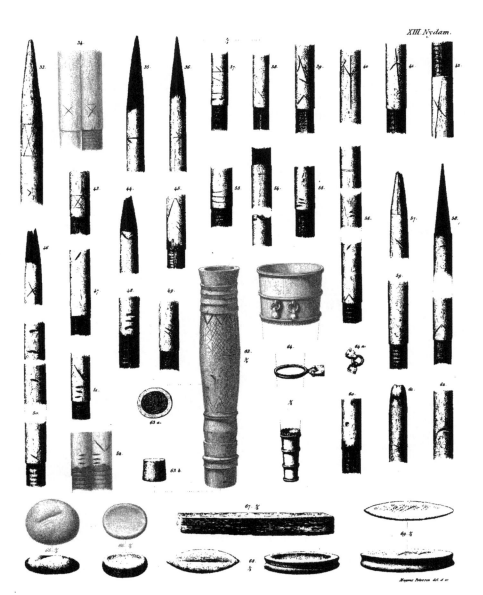

Magnus Petersen del. & sc.

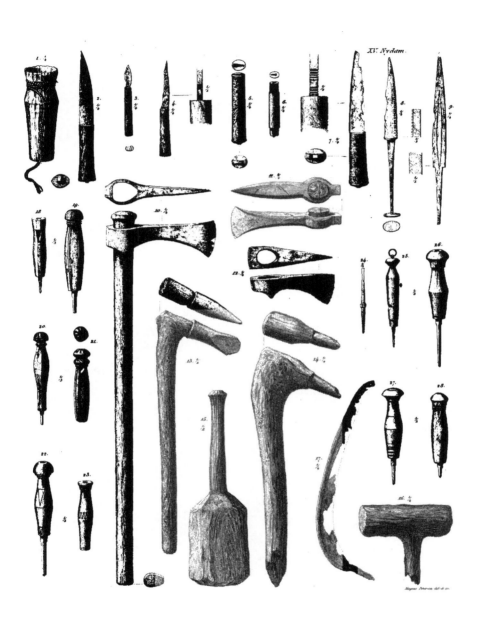